MW00799208

Who Is African-American –
What Does It Mean?

Plus

Let's Talk About Race
Relations in America

M ARK J. P ALOMINO

PublishAmerica
Baltimore

First printing

ISBN: 1-4241-2384-4
PUBLISHED BY PUBLISHAMERICA, LLLP
www.publishamerica.com
Baltimore

Printed in the United States of America

So who are you? Are you American or African-American?

Is African-American a race?

If African-American is a nationality, then all Americans would have to be called African-Americans because all citizens of the same country share the same nationality.

Reactive racism is just as bad as active racism—as the Holy Scriptures tell us, not to render evil for evil (1 Thessalonians 5: 15).

Mark J. Palomino

This book is dedicated to my mother, Adassa, who has taught me to love everyone with agape love. My mother and I had the most wonderful relationship a mother and son could have; and she gave me enough love to last me for a lifetime. She was the most unselfish person I had ever known, and because of her I have been the recipient of many wonderful blessings. Over the years, many people have told me how kind she had been to them, and in return, they have been kind to me. It is on this premise of recycled love that I believe we can accomplish many great feats as a nation and as a people.

Acknowledgments

First and foremost I would like to thank God for inspiring me to write this book. Without God's inspiration and guidance I could not have written this book. I would like to specially thank my cousin Marlyn, who was most instrumental in the completion of this book. Without her continued help and support this book could not have been written at this time. Thanks to all my friends and relatives who rendered moral support and who served as patient critiquers during the writing process. In no particular order some of these people are: Devon Nunes, Errol (Vito) Carvalho, Cassandra Palomino, Bryan Nunes, Michelle Marsh, Sylvia Allen, Gabrielle Williams, Dr. Patricia Williams, Glenroy Williams, Neil Humphrey, Uwaine Frazer, H. Anthony Burke, and Crawford (Bobo) West. I would also like to thank the many people in Atlanta, Philadelphia, Boston, New York, and elsewhere overseas who took the time to dialogue with me—my sincere gratitude to all.

To: Kellie

Thanks for your technical support Wish you all great things for future endeavors

Contents

Introduction

America is a land of hope—a land where dreams can come through for anyone who has dreams and is willing to pursue them. Unlike many parts of the world where a dream remains only a dream for the ordinary people, in America anyone can fulfill his or her dream. Sometimes, however, in order to fulfill one's dream, one has to climb high mountains and cross many rivers before one can see one's dream off at a distance. At times one has to be persistent in order to realize one's dream because dreams can be illusive—just when everything seems promising, life throws a detour. America is a land replete with an abundance of opportunities. Most opportunities, nonetheless, are not just lying in green pastures waiting to be picked up. They have to be sought after diligently.

Although many potential opportunities lie waiting to be found, there exist many Americans—black American people—who believe that only certain people can find them. Many black Americans today live in a delusional state of subserviency, believing that this country is only for the "white man," and that they are still bound by the "white man's" chains, unable to achieve anything they desire, or fulfill any desired dream. Many educational opportunities lie wasting while many black American people go adrift in a sea of ignorance. Far too many black people have bought into the lie that black people are not as smart or intelligent as people of other races. As a result, black people tend to show more respect for people of other races than they show for their own race, in this materialistic society. Black America needs a revival to shine a new light of hope and to give a new sense of direction toward true liberty and the pursuit of oneness.

This book is written to serve as an impetus to the reconditioning of the minds of Americans who insist on remaining in the classroom, but who refuse to enroll and become active participants in the pursuit of true liberty. This book is not meant to engender any feelings of hostility toward anyone, and is definitely not meant to cause any perturbation among Americans—especially between white and black Americans. One of its purposes is to shine light into the darkness, so that everyone can see clearly and avoid agitation due to constant bombardment of ignorance and malevolent acts of humanity.

The main purpose of this book, however, is to argue the point that all Americans should be treated as equal and legitimate members of society. That is conceivably unachievable when only some Americans are perceived as veritable Americans while others are considered "X" Americans. In American society, only white Americans seem to be considered veritable Americans—everyone else is an "X" American. The letter "X" in itself usually connotes "wrong." To be facetious, it seems to be that only white is right and everyone else is wrong. If the matter is taken seriously, it seems as if we live in a society that still condones white supremacy, yet hypocritically declares democracy. Social equality is one of the tenets of democracy, but in America a blind man can see clearly that there is no such thing as social equality. Another thing, when did God create a third gender?

The social structure in America is so complex that Americans try to politically correct everything to appease the masses. However, in the face of political correctness, some things seem to become more complex. One of these complexities is the absurd three-gender system that America has developed: men, women and minorities. Just considering this three-gender system also proves the foregoing notion that America condones white supremacy. This three-gender system is what the media uses to categorize Americans. It seems to imply that there is no significant gender within the minorities group. In other words, as far as the minorities group is concerned, everyone is just one big insignificant lump. Those white Americans who seem to believe that they are the only legitimate Americans or legitimate humans, need to shed their presumptuous clothing of haughtiness and embrace godliness in which they will attain true liberty.

In America we are also confused with race, ethnicity, culture, and nationality—we do not seem to know which is which. Some Americans of black African descent have chosen to be referred to as African-Americans. Yet, from the many people that I have asked the true meaning of the term, none seems to know whether it is a race, a nationality, a culture, or an ethnic group. Additionally, with the exception of white Americans, all Americans are considered X-Americans. The original people of America are dubbed Native-Americans to show that not even they are claimants to the true title—Americans. The question that I cannot wait to ask is: Who is a Native-American? If you were born in a particular country, are you not a native of that country? So, if you were born in America, are you not a Native-American? If you are not an American native, then what would you be a native of? This would mean that you are without a country; and that means all Americans—black, white or whomever—except the veritable Native-Americans.

A quick suggestion: The only categories that seem to make any sense would be to refer to all born Americans as Native-Americans; however, this should be necessary only as a distinguishing tool, since within America we have a need for specific categories of people. So, Americans could be described more accurately as black American native, white American native, etc. The so-called Native-Americans could be referred to—only as a distinguishing tool—as Original-American Native. Naturalized American citizens could be referred to simply as naturalized Americans.

The main theme of this book is to discuss the term African-American. We will try to find the real meaning of the term, if it exists, and later show that it is a fallacy to use it to describe black people in America. We show that it is an ambiguous term that can probably be more harmful than helpful to the American black populace. We ask if the term African-American is a race, a culture, a nationality or an ethnic group. Each category is dealt with separately, and the conclusion gives the final argument concerning each one.

Chapter seven gives a summary of race relations in America from a subjective point of view. Most of the chapter is based on the author's own perspective. Also included in chapter seven are the author's theories on race relations from a retrospective point of view; and the consequences of the slave and slave-master relationship. The slave / slave-master relationship is taken into account when considering the current state of affairs of black people in America; and the antagonistic relationship between white and black Americans. We introduce a condition—the *Puppy Dog Mentality Syndrome* or PDMS—that the slaves theoretically developed by association with the white slave master; and that has transcended the generations, and has apparently taken root. The slave-slave master relationship is also taken into account when discussing the hatred that black people share among themselves, and the built-up insecurities resulting in disunity and despair. We also talk a little about racism from a somewhat introspective point of view, while introducing two theoretical types of racism. We include some perspectives from interviews with white Americans and various other people. We ask some white Americans why they harbor so much hatred for black people in America, but have different feelings when they are among black people in foreign countries.

It is hoped that the contents of this book will serve to enlighten all its readers on the topics discussed, and to encourage harmony not only between white and black Americans, but harmony among black people themselves and all other peoples.

Chapter 1

Who is African-American?

I have tried very hard to remember the first time I heard the term *African-American,* but I cannot seem to put a date on it. I do not recall hearing it in the eighties but I surely could not hide from it in the nineties, and it is ubiquitous today. I continuously wonder if I am unique, or if there are other people in America who are just disgusted with hearing this term being used liberally every day, to describe American people of black African descent. I have become sensitized to the term in such a way that every time I hear it mentioned, I automatically tune out the speaker—whether on the radio or on television or in person.

I always thought that it is the most ludicrous and discrediting contribution to the American black populace. I have a strong sense of resentment for the *African-American* term that is not likely to change, because I view it as a compressive force—a force that keeps one confined. Once under the influence of such a force, there is no likely room for expansion. I also see it as an *oppressive* force because its benefits, if there are any, are very limiting and are not universal.

Why do Americans, born and raised in the only society that they can call their own and to which they are accustomed and call their home, refer to themselves as if they are foreigners in their own country? Americans who are of black African descent are the only Americans who on a daily basis wear an "X" prefix to their American nationality. No other racial group in America does that. White Americans do not refer to themselves as European Americans. As a matter of fact, I could not find a definition for *European-American* in a particular dictionary, which had a definition for African-American. Obviously, as far as that dictionary is concerned, there is no such thing as a European-American because white Americans do not consider themselves anything but Americans.

I have never heard a white American say "well, as a European American I ......" Americans of black African descent are the only Americans who from sunup to sundown refer to themselves as "X-Americans," while everybody else is just American. I do not think that I can watch the news on television or listen to the radio on any given day without hearing the *African-American* term within an hour, or several times before the day is over. I have never heard—not even once—anyone in the news media refer to any American as European-American; and only on special occasions will the "X-American" *label* be used to describe Americans from other racial or ethnic groups.

Black American people are very much Americans as all the other peoples of the American society, but make up the only fraction that is generally identified as "X-Americans." It may be all right for American black people to identify themselves as descendants of Africans; but American black people (just as black people in other countries outside the content of Africa), are not Africans. Being of African descent does not mean that you are African, in the same way that being of European descent does not mean that you are European. Black people in other western countries, for example, identify themselves as natives of their country of birth. They do not use an "X" prefix as Americans do.

One white American that I interviewed told me that black American people call themselves African-Americans because they are trying to find an identity. After giving that much thought, I wondered why on God's earth would American black people be trying to find an identity. Black American people have among themselves some of the most prominent people throughout the entire world. Black American people have excelled in just about everything in which they are involved, and sometimes far beyond other people in most other countries; and have had tremendous influences on people in every corner of the world. The main problem, however, is that the greatness of black American people is not expressed in relatively great numbers within the United States. Consequently, this makes black American people vulnerable to prejudice and discrimination. Let us not forget also that black American people are some of the most admired, idolized, respected, and emulated people in the world. So why should black American people be trying to find an identity when everyone else is trying to be like them?

As all the peoples of the west, we are people of the new world. We are black people who are descendants of black Africans from the continent of Africa; but we are descendants only, and many of us are mixed with other races. Therefore, our ancestral roots are one in many. However, as black people we embrace our ancestral African root, but we are not Africans. Therefore, American black people should identify themselves as Americans only, and not as African-Americans. Black people in America can trace their American roots many generations back, not unlike Americans of European and Asian descent.

Americans of European descent have been living in this country for so long now, they claim no ties to Europe and definitely do not claim to be Europeans. They have planted their roots so deeply in American soil that they are unshakable; and everywhere they go they are recognized as Americans. People nowadays do not normally think of white Americans as people who are originally from Europe—of course not. So why should black Americans constantly view themselves as people from Africa? White Americans claim only America as their own—and proud of it—as they chant "I'm proud to be an American." It is imperative to be proud of your country, especially the country that shares your family history. Therefore, as Americans, black people need to wake from their states of despondency and dispel the delusion of tenantry. Other western countries are no different from America in that they are an amalgamation of people from many different origins.

I remember a scenario when I was involved in undergraduate scientific research in college. A white female graduate student—who was a resident of the laboratory where I was doing my research—had left to teach one of her classes. While she was away, one of her students—a white male—from another of her classes came looking for her. When she returned later I told her that a European-American student was looking for her. She replied, "Who was he, does he speak with an accent?" So, as far as this graduate student is concerned, a European-American is a person who speaks with an accent. In other words, a European-American is a foreigner.

It made me wonder what this same graduate student and other white Americans thought of an African-American. Therefore, I asked many white Americans exactly that—what they thought of Americans who called themselves African-Americans. Surprisingly, almost one hundred percent (100%) of them thought it was ridiculous, and thought that black Americans are just as much Americans as they are. It is amazing how so many white Americans think alike, and most think that black Americans are trying to find an identity.

Many white Americans do not know much about their ancestral origins, any more than their black American compatriots. However, everyone is quite aware that black people in America are descendants of Africans and that white people are descendants of Europeans. Yet, white Americans accept the "Land of the Free" as their home. As far as they are concerned, that is all the identity they need.

I think that it should be insulting to black American people when someone says that they are searching for an identity. Their ancestral origin is quite obvious and who black American people are is quite obvious too. Black American people belong to this country in the same way that black people form the Caribbean countries belong to those countries; but black people from the Caribbean countries identify themselves with their country of birth. A black Dominican who is very much of black African descent as an American, identifies himself as Dominican—that is it. So why should there be an identity problem as far as black American people are concerned?

Black American people are not tenants in America and should never feel inferior to anyone here. Some say that they want to be called African-Americans because they do not want to be called colored. Not wanting to be called colored does not mean that one has to be called something else. How about just American; or if a race description is required, then, how about just black? White Americans do not use *Americans of European descent* as their race. So why should black people identify themselves as *Americans of African descent?*

Nevertheless, to identify oneself as *American of African descent* when necessary is probably more appropriate than to constantly identify oneself as an African-American.

No one should have the right to make up *labels* to espouse everyone involuntarily. I believe though, that black people resent being called colored because that is a *tag* that was placed on them by Americans of European descent and colored may sound like something dirty. I also believe that black people do not like being called colored because they reciprocate by calling Americans of European descent white people; and of course white sounds like something clean and pure—especially from the connotation in most literature.

Therefore, what we have here is something that sounds superior and another that sounds inferior; or one thing that sounds clean and the other dirty. Yet, the situation does not have to be viewed that way. First of all, it seems as if *black* people focus too much on *white* people and are apt to give them undue respect; the kind of respect that propagates the slave and slave master association. Some back people, it seems, do not realize that white people are just people too, with every basic need as every other human being. One could look at the picture from a different angle and discover something that might have been hidden by shadows of subserviency, or something that illuminates when light strikes it. If we look at things in terms of relative opposites then our perspectives might be different. For example: If Americans of European descent refer to Americans of African descent as colored, then the relative opposite of colored is colorless or non-colored. Therefore, if Americans of African descent refer to Americans of European descent as colorless people or non-colored people instead of white people then the picture would look much different.

So then, what we would have are colored people and colorless people; people of color and people without color; or colored people and non-colored people. These are relative opposites that make more sense than colored people and white people. These are the kinds of comparisons that we should have learned in kindergarten. Without relative opposites one is led to believe that having color is a bad thing, but people without supposed color spend numerous hours in the sun trying to get what they consider color. So having color must be very good; and of course we know that people of so-called color are very beautiful, just as well as people without so-called color.

It is not necessary for one to trample over another in order for one to feel good about oneself; and black people do not have to hate white people in order to feel empowered or self-assured. Moreover, there are too many black people who behave as though white people are the parents of black people. They tend to believe that it is the responsibility of white Americans to provide their every need. Not so! The past we cannot change but the future we sure can. Therefore, it is time we started focusing on ourselves, not only as individuals but as a people, and not only in words but in deeds. It is time black American people started seeing themselves as legitimate Americans blessed with all kinds of gifts and talents that can only be harnessed by togetherness. If we are Americans then let us say so.

In one of his addresses during the presidential campaign, Senator John Kerry talked about African-American votes, but he never talked about European-American votes. When referring to white Americans, one simply says Americans. Are black Americans, then, perceived as real Americans as are white Americans? Or are black Americans perceived as special cases—like aliens—people with special needs? Why is it that America seems to be divided into Americans and African-Americans?

In the Olympics we compete as Americans, and in wars we fight together as Americans. So, why are we not all Americans when at home? Many black Americans seem to have a problem with being called black, but these same people do not have a problem calling Americans of European descent white people. The fact that most people outside the United States do not normally differentiate between white and black Americans—all are considered Yankees—should be conclusive evidence that an American is an American irrespective of color or race.

Many people in foreign countries who never traveled to the United States do not know anything about "African-American." They know only "American." A person in a foreign country looking at the beautiful people in *Ebony* magazine, for example, sees only Americans. However, he or she may read about African-Americans in the magazine and thus become sensitized and confused.

Technically speaking, Americans are all peoples of North America, South America, Central America and the Caribbean; Americans are all the peoples of the Americas. However, we have come to accept the colloquial usage of *Americans* as people from the United Sates of America. So, it means that if you were born in the United States of America, you are an American and nothing else. America is a culturally and ethnically diverse society with just about every culture and ethnic group one can imagine represented throughout the different regions of the country. Of course, America is also racially divided into all the respective races; not just black and white peoples. Black and white Americans, nonetheless, have traditionally grabbed most of the media attention for one reason or another; but let us not forget that there are other peoples that constitute the American society.

On the one hand white Americans seem to be very proud of their American heritage and feel very strongly bonded to their American nationality. They love their homeland and nobody can tell them that they are anything but Americans. Black Americans, on the other hand, seem to continue to feel as though America is not their homeland and thus feel the need to embrace an obscure immigrant-like identity. I believe that this assumed identity is an unnecessary destructive device to the psyche of black people living in America. It is the embodiment of retrogression.

There are many Americans who are non-black or non-white who are highly offended when they are referred to as anything other than Americans. They take very seriously their American citizenship and are very proud to be Americans. There is one particular scenario that I recall. When I was a student in college I remember asking a fellow student—whom I thought was Korean, but was not quite sure—where he was from. He replied "I'm American." I did not take him seriously because I thought he knew what I actually meant. So I asked again, "Yeah! But what's your ancestry?" I could see the paleness of his face disappearing as his cheeks became flushed and his angered eyes fixed unto mine like a cat ready for an attack. He replied this time more fervently, "I'm American!"

That student—whom many may dub Asian-American—was quite aware, I am sure, that his ancestors are Asians; but it was more important to him that I knew that he was American. He did not wish to share his ancestral roots with me at the time, and as far as being Asian is concerned, that is obvious to the rest of the world. As far as he was concerned, the only thing that I needed to know was that he is American.

I had a little problem initially with the answer that the student gave me, because I thought that maybe he was ashamed of his ancestral origin—as some children of immigrants tend to be. However, later with reasoning, my perspective of the situation changed. Now I can think of him as a person who demonstrated individualism and one who took pride in his American heritage. He also did not choose to wear an "X-American" *label,* which I found quite intriguing. Maybe he did not care to wear an "X-American" label because he might have noticed that his white friends were not wearing one. In spite of any negative thought that I might have had about that student initially, he had every right to defend his legitimate title as an American.

Why then do American black people who are an integral part of the American society, feel the need to keep reminding everyone that they are of African descent, as if it is not obvious; and disregarding the struggles of those who were lucky to receive only a status of three-fifths of a person, much less full citizenship. As a matter of fact, anyone who looks at a picture of the great Dr. Martin Luther King does not have to ask if his ascendants are from the content of Africa.

Everyone knows that the majority of black people in America are of African descent, just as much as we know that white Americans are of European descent. So one's sense of belonging should not really be affected by how one arrived here. Whether we arrived here by the *Mayflower*, as indentured servants, slaves, or immigrants of later times; the fact is that we are all part of the "Home of the Brave." Being a part of the "Home of the Brave" is worth treasuring if we are going to have a cohesive American society where everyone is treated with equality irrespective of race, color, ethnicity or any other factor.

America is not a homogeneous society; therefore, regardless of the racial differences, an American is an American. Every law-abiding American regardless of race should feel as though he or she is a valuable unit of the American society, and should never feel as if he or she is an inferior unit for any reason whatsoever. America was built and became great by the sweat of people of many races, including the black race, of which was the "head corner stone." So black American people should be proud to know that they are a major part of the building blocks of this nation without which, who knows what kind of America we would have today. Black American people are legitimate citizens of America, deserving of all the rights and privileges; many have made great sacrifices so this could be so. Hence I do believe that this is a civil right that should not be surrendered by any means, and definitely not in the name of African-Americanism.

So who are you? Are you American or African-American? I often wonder if there are serious deleterious effects due to this *African-Americanism*. How does African-Americanism affect Americans of black African descent? I have found that there are many black people in America who are offended by being referred to as African-Americans. Some may be naturalized citizens who believe that their true identity is lost in African-Americanism; or they could be any born American who feels illegitimate. For some of these people it does not matter if they are originally from the continent of Africa or if they were born in the United States to immigrants from the continent of Africa or any foreign country.

It is interesting to know that Americans who are originally from the continent of Africa (naturalized citizens or residents), or those born to immigrants of the same, do not refer to themselves as African-Americans. It proves to be a term that they all despise. Most Americans who were born to recent immigrants from the continent of Africa usually identify themselves as either Americans of Nigerian descent, for example, or just plain African. Many of them prefer to identify themselves with the respective country of origin of their parents; then they will add that they were born here. However, I have yet to hear any of them use the African-American terminology to identify themselves. Although they are usually very proud of their African heritage, they all seem to find the term African-American laughable.

Americans who resent the African-American *label* do so not because they are ashamed of their African ancestry—and there is no reason why they should—but because they see no nexus between them and the term African-American. A lot of people never heard the term until they arrived in the United States—to them it is alien—so, it is difficult and downright ludicrous to make such a drastic change in one's being. These people also have no affinity for the African-American *label* because they wear with them every day, their cultural and their national pride from back home; even though they are quite aware, however, that sometimes they have to wear it involuntarily due to their color and the need for political correctness in America.

Black immigrants are apt to see themselves as people completely different from native black people. As far as they are concerned, native Black Americans are the ones who are African-Americans (because they allegedly assumed the *title); but not them. In fact, many black immigrants tend not to see much at all in common with native black Americans, especially because of the difference in identification—whether racial, ethnic or otherwise. Some native black people feel the same way about black immigrants—they see them as aliens, and as people who came here to take their jobs. This difference between the two groups usually results in division and segregation among the common people.

Why do black immigrants have a problem identifying with native black people? Could it be because they do not want to associate themselves with the term African-American, which in general they eschew? Why do native black people see black immigrants as people so distant from themselves? Why do so many native black people, especially in the inner cities, allow themselves to be utterly disrespected by immigrants running corner stores? Why don't these native black people walk with their heads held high and demand the respect that they deserve as Americans living in America—their homeland! Respect, of course, does not come by force or by begging—

it is an earned process based on cumulative diligent service. Therefore, with time and much effort and much progressive change, one can gain the desired respect.

Foreigners generally do not treat white Americans with the same level of disrespect as they do black Americans. Neither do foreigners tend to treat white Americans as if they do not belong here; but then White Americans do not consider themselves "X-Americans" either. So then, could there be a resultant psychological, socio-economic, emotional or social impact in calling Americans African-Americans? Is African-American a race, a culture, an ethnic group or a nationality? Is it politically correct to refer to all black people in America or black people in the rest of the world as African-Americans?

Americans of black African descent could legitimately be called African-Americans, in a casual way, the same way that we refer to other Americans according to their ethnicity. We often use the terms Italian-American, Irish-American, Polish-American, etc. to refer to one's ethnicity—to tell one's ancestral roots, so to speak. Yet, the problem with referring to an American as an African-American is that Africa is not a country—it is a continent. There are many countries in Africa, and I am sure that they are ethnically different form one another. Ethiopians and Nigerians are noticeably different in terms of language and behavioral customs among other things—the same way that Italians are different from Germans. Besides, Americans of black African descent tend to use the term African-Americans to indicate their race, not their ethnicity. On job application forms, for example, one normally sees: African-American / Black; White / Caucasian; …. One never sees Italian-American, Irish-American or any other ethnic group. So here we can see that one term is being used as an ethnic indicator while the other term is being used as a race indicator. The term African-American is used as a race indicator not only on job application forms of course, but in all aspects of society.

It should be understood that the term African-American is neither a culture nor an ethnic group—as we shall establish later; and it is neither a race nor a nationality, which we shall also establish later. Therefore, we shall declare that it is inappropriate to indiscriminately use the term African-Americans to refer to all Americans who just happen to be black.

It is obvious that not all Europeans are the same. A Russian is very different from a Dutch in many ways; and we cannot treat a Frenchman as if he is British, because ethnically and culturally they are different. In like manner, black American people are very different from one another. A black American of Nigerian descent is very different culturally and in many other ways from a black American of Cuban or Puerto Rican descent. So why is it that all black people in general are lumped in the same *"African-American basket"?* Furthermore, not all Africans are black, so why is the term African-American restricted to black people?

Should non-black Americans of North African descent (people originally from North African countries such as Algeria and Libya) be offended by being called African-Americans—because they are not really black (since *African-Americans* is reserved for black American people); or should they be offended because they are not considered African-Americans—and they are indeed of African descent? Additionally, are Native black Americans (including but not limited to Americans born to non-immigrant parents) the only ones who deserve the *African-American* title? Or are all black people in America automatically perceived as African-Americans?

This brings us to the burning question of who is really African-American and why do American people choose to alienate themselves from their own country? American people who call themselves African-Americans are delusional, if they think that this is not their country. I have often heard black American people say that everyone has a country to return to except for them (the same thing that I have heard some white Americans say of black Americans); but if everyone is coming to your country then obviously they have a country to return to. If black American people were the ones immigrating then they would have a country to return to just as the people who are immigrating here—and your country is the one where most people want to come.

The majority of white Americans are no more Europeans than black Americans are Africans. If white people can return to Europe, then black people can return to Africa. Any black person right now, if he or she so chooses, can assume domicile in any African country. As a matter of fact, any American can choose to live anywhere he or she decides. So why should black American people feel as if they are aliens in their own country, and yearn for a country to return to? In your country, you should be called Americans, not African-Americans. The term African-American, as far as I am concerned, infers second-class citizenship status and connotes pseudo-American. It is really preposterous that Americans of black African descent are the only Americans who insist on wearing an identity *label* as if to say they would be inconspicuous without the *label.*

However, I believe that quite the contrary is true. You become inconspicuous if you have no value; and you have no value if you have no power; and you have no power if you are disregarded; and you are disregarded if you are devalued. Devaluation can assume more than one form, the worst of which is psychological self-devaluation. To voluntarily place oneself in a second-class status, psychologically, is a crippling form of self-devaluation.

Currently in the United States, one has to be a citizen to acquire certain positions. Will Americans psychologically renounce their citizenship by placing themselves in a psychologically inferior stratosphere? If one should ask oneself the question—Who am I; am I a citizen of the United States of America? If I am, then why am I not recognized as an American—with no "X" prefix—as other Americans? Why am I being called by a different name?

When Senator John Kerry addressed a black American audience during his presidential campaign he mentioned African-American votes, but when he addressed white Americans he addressed them as Americans. President Bush and others, including black American people themselves also use the term African-American to define American black people. As far as I am concerned, the term African-American is very ambiguous and disparaging. I also believe that it is a term that the majority of black people in America did not choose for themselves and one which they do not quite comprehend. So, again I have to ask the question, who is African-American?

Chapter 2

Is African-American a Race?

According to the typical job application form in America, the term African-American undoubtedly designates race. The question of one's race normally comes in a format typical of the one below.

1. White/Non-Hispanic
2. African-American/Black
3. Hispanic
4. Asian/Pacific Islander
5. Other

There are other formats depending on the particular form and its purpose; but this format seems to be more common than others.

Incidentally, a lot of people usually have no problem filling out the typical job application form until they reach the section on *race*. This can be the most challenging part of the form for some people because it appears to be either too exclusive or ambiguous. It can also be unpleasant because some people have difficulty with exactly where they fit in, and so they do not know which option to select. If number two above is taken into consideration, is it implying that someone is either African-American or black; or is it implying that African-American and black are synonymous? If someone is either African-American or black, then who exactly is African-American and who is black? If African-American and black are synonymous, does it mean that if you are black then you are automatically African-American? In effect, that would imply that all black people everywhere would be considered African-Americans, which is preposterous.

Additionally, what if you are black and you are of Hispanic/Latino heritage? There is no option for Hispanic/Black; or even for Hispanic/White for that matter. However, there is an option for White/Non-Hispanic, which in itself implies that there is indeed a category for White/Hispanic. However, since there is no category for White/Hispanic or Black/Hispanic, this seems to give the impression that all Hispanic or Latino peoples are the same.

One needs to be aware that in the Hispanic or Latino community there are all kinds of people from different racial origins. It may be easy to gain an insight of this notion if one can accept the fact that the English language is spoken by a vast number of people of different races. No one ever says "You speak English, so you cannot be black—you must be English." So, why is it so difficult for so many people to understand the equivalent for the Spanish language? Many people seem to believe that if you speak Spanish then you are not black—you are Spanish.

There are many people who believe that if you are from a Spanish-speaking country, or of Spanish heritage, then, that is what you are—Spanish. They do not think that you can speak Spanish and be black at the same time, in the same way that you can speak English and be black simultaneously. One's native language is not an indication of one's race. There are many black people in Spanish-speaking countries such as Panama, Puerto Rico, Cuba, Venezuela and the Dominican Republic—to name a few. Some people often refer to Spanish-speaking people as "Spanish." The only people who are literally "Spanish" are those people from Spain; and you can be from Spain and be black too, just as you can be from America and be black. The same goes for speaking Spanish and being white simultaneously.

As far as the job application form is concerned, black people who are originally from the English-speaking Caribbean or from other English-speaking countries outside of America, and who are of non-Hispanic or Latino descent, normally choose option 5. They normally choose option 5 because they are usually dissatisfied with option 2. They generally eschew the term *African-American* and prefer not to be identified as such. A lot of immigrants in general are apt to select option 5, except for black people of Hispanic or Latino descent who normally choose option 3 because they are indeed of Spanish heritage and feel more closely related to option 3 than option 2. The actual consequences of black people in America selecting option 5 can have serious political and economic consequences because of misrepresentation.

According to *The Columbia Encyclopedia*, Sixth Edition, 2001, the human race is divided into three main categories: Caucasoid, Mongoloid, and Negroid, based on limiting criteria of traits such as skin pigmentation, color and form of hair, shape of head, stature, and form of nose. Without delving deeper into the definition of these terms, let us just admit that none of us has ever seen any of these terms on a job application form, as a *race* description. Therefore, let us be truthful and say that when we think of race what usually comes to mind is White, Black, Asian, etc. Regardless of what we may consider race to be, one thing we do know for sure—is that whatever our race, we cannot change it. That is to say, we are always what we are, regardless of where we are. The question therefore, is—**Is African-American a race?** An equally significant question is—**Who is really African-American?** Let us deal with the latter question first.

According to the *Webster's New World College Dictionary*, "African-American" means *a Black American person*. The problem with this definition, however, is that it is very ambiguous. Who is a *Black American person?* Does the term *African-American* apply only to black people who were born in America; or does it include all black people who are citizens of America (including naturalized Americans); or does it mean all black people in general who are living in America?

If in general, only some black people in America are considered African-Americans, then, on a day-by-day basis, can anyone distinguish between those who are African-Americans and those who are black but who are not really African-Americans? These are legitimate questions, as I myself have noticed that the term appears to be used indiscriminately to describe everyone in America who happens to look black, in almost all cases. It is used to describe just about anyone irrespective of mixed races or whether one is an American citizen or not.

It seems also that many people are earnestly trying to be politically correct, but unfortunately not many of us are well initiated in the confusing realm of racial political correctness. Therefore, some people tend to use the term liberally without consideration of its implications. As a result of their desire to placate the masses, they have extended the use of the term, with good intentions, I believe, to include black people in foreign countries as well. I once heard a White American say, "Oh! The African-American is in the lead," referring to Sammy Sosa (a Dominican) when he was facing off with Mark McGuire—a white American—in baseball. I also heard an American student, while in Santo Domingo, referred to a Dominican professor as "the African-American female." He thought of course that he was being politically correct because the Dominican professor looked black—in his eyes anyway—and as far as he is concerned that is what black people are— African-Americans.

The term African-American nowadays is ubiquitous and is used, it seems, to describe everyone in America who looks black. It is being used without exemption to describe everyone of black African descent or any mixture thereof. What is worse is the way many white Americans and other non-black Americans have come to use it liberally to describe black people in America. They think it is a term that all black people in America have accepted as a new and politically correct identity. Apparently there are millions of Americans who do not realize that not all Americans (black Americans) think of themselves as African-Americans, and who do not whish to be called African-Americans under any circumstance.

There are many black people who have immigrated to the United States from countries in Africa and other parts of the world. In their homelands they might have been known as Nigerians, Jamaicans, Cubans, Guyanese, French, etcetera; however, now that they are in America, their status changes. They are now seen as someone different from what they are used to. They are forced to wear the *African-American label* that is somewhat like a *monkey* on their backs.

Sometimes they are not even aware that the *monkey* is there until they are being stared at and wonder why people are staring at them. They have lost their true identity and have become someone else, against their will. They have to carry the burden of the *monkey* every day because it is the politically correct thing to do.

There are many Americans who decry carrying this burden but they have no choice in the matter. Why? Because everyone gets caught up in political correctness; but unfortunately sometimes things seem to become obscure in the process. Not to mention how presumptuous and foolish some people can be. They pick up a little catch-phrase and turn around and apply it aimlessly to everything. How can you go to the Dominican Republic and refer to Dominicans as *African-Americans*— that is so ridiculous—these people know nothing of such a term. Dominicans consider themselves nothing but Dominicans, not unlike people in England who consider themselves English. People in other countries do not refer to themselves as *African-Americans.*

America is not the only country with black people who are descendants of black Africans after the remnants of slavery. However, in other countries, people who are of black African descent are usually proud of their native heritage—although they are also well aware of their African ancestry just as American people are. They do not need to identify themselves with a prefix. It does not matter either if they are of mixed races, they are quite aware of their African roots. Yet, they accept as their own, the country in which they were born and identify themselves with that country.

Only in America things appear to become complicated. American people who are black seem to be discontented with being just Americans (unlike their white compatriots who will never answer to European-Americans). Black American people have to constantly remind the world that they are of African descent as if it is not obvious; and worse of all use the term as if it is the official and universal *label* for all black people.

I once heard a woman called in on a radio talk show, and identified herself as a woman of *African-American* descent—as her opening line. I thought to myself that this *African-American* thing is really getting out of hand. I could understand if the woman had said that she is

African-American, because she is indeed an American and she is black; and that is the *label* that is being *pinned* on black people in America. However, how does someone get to be an American of African-American descent? I think that we have to come to a consensus and decide what the real meaning is—if there is one—of the term *African-American.* Or we could come to an agreement that the term African-American is without a doubt a fallacy, and that nobody is really African-American.

Let us deal with the question: **Is African-American a race**?

As mentioned above, one cannot change one's race. Therefore, if *African-American* is a race, what happens then, if an American who is considered African-American decides to move from America to France and become a French citizen? Is this person still an African-American? Or does this person become an African-American-French? Of course, the term African-American-French looks like a German word that probably has something to do with the United Nations. It would not make any sense to anyone either, especially because it is not a true description of anyone's race—just seems like a group of hyphenated related countries. Additionally, one can clearly see the nonsense of the whole thing if one considers that in France, for example, black people do not consider themselves African-Americans— they are French.

Consider this: what would one consider a black British person? Surely he or she cannot be called African-American; not according to the above definition (a black American person). However, he or she is still black. So what we have here is inconsistency in racial description. This can only lead to ultimate confusion as a person moves from one place to another. One's racial identity should be invariable. That is to say, whatever one's race, it has to be constant regardless of one's geographic location. For example, a white man in Japan is still a white man, even though he could be German or Russian or any other nationally. Mere geography does not change his race.

If the term African-American is to be used as a racial description for black people, then it cannot be exclusive. It would have to appropriately classify all black people and be constant throughout. Therefore, a black person in England or France would also have to be African-American. Hence, since the term *African-American* cannot racially classify all black people in America or the world, it is therefore, not a legitimate racial term and should not be used on job application forms or anywhere else to racially describe people.

If one thinks seriously about the term African-American, it should become quite clear that it is really preposterous that Americans choose to espouse such a separatist means of identification. This separatist identification has apparently become the consequence of more confusion among the common people than any realistic observed benefit. American people—black people—seem to be so confused that they can no longer think of themselves as a unit. Some say they are black; some say they are African-Americans; some say they are Afro-Americans; and some are just plain clueless. I have interviewed many people of different races, in the streets of America and also in different countries, asking them various questions concerning the term African-American. Talking with these people served as proof of the state of confusion among American black folks as well as other peoples. Excerpts from some of these interviews are as follow:

1. A 72-year-old woman in an Atlanta supermarket:
Me: "What do you call yourself—American or African-American?"
Her: "Well, I guess African-American."
Me: "Why do you consider yourself African-American?"
Her: "Well, that's what they call us."
Me: "Who are they?"
Her: "You know—white people."
Me: "I don't think that white people are the ones who started calling black people African-Americans."
Her: "Well, I don't know, all I know is that's what they call us."
Me: "Do you mind being called African-American?"
Her: "Well, I never really thought much about it to tell you the truth."
Me: "Thanks for sharing your time with me."
Her: "Don't mention it."

2. A young black female in an Atlanta supermarket:

Me: "What do you call yourself—American or African-American?"

Her: "I consider myself black."

Me: "But what do you think about the term African-American?"

Her: "I hate it. I don't consider myself African-American because I'm not from Africa. I'm from right here in Atlanta."

Me: "Do you think Black American people should call themselves African-Americans?"

Her: "I think it's stupid. They are not immigrants form Africa and besides, they don't even know anything about Africa."

Me: "There's so much I'd like to talk with you about, but I can see that you are in a hurry. Thanks anyway for your time."

Her: "Wish I could spend more time with you. Thanks!"

3. An older lady in Kingston, Jamaica:

Me: "What do you think of American people who refer to themselves as African- Americans?"

Her: "I think it's stupid. They are Americans, not African-Americans. We here in Jamaica don't call ourselves African-Jamaicans. We are just Jamaicans."

A white American male in Santo Domingo, Dominican Republic:

Me: "What do you think of Black Americans referring to themselves as African-Americans?"

He: "I think it's ridiculous. It seams like just another tool to further segregate themselves. I don't think of them as African-Americans, but if that's what they feel happy with that's their choice."

A black American male in an Atlanta shopping plaza:

Me: "What do you consider yourself—American or Africa-American?"

He: "I consider myself African-American."

Me: "Why do you consider yourself African-American?"

He: "Because that's where my ancestors came from."

*Me: "But you are an American. Why do you want to be referred to
as if you are an immigrant?"*
He: "Because I want to identify with Africa."
*Me: "How come White Americans don't refer to themselves as
European-Americans?"*
*He: "That's their problem if they don't want to identify with
Europe, but I want to identify with Africa."*
Me: "Thanks! I don't want to take up any more of your time."
He: "Take it easy, man."

A white American male in Atlanta
*Me: "What do you think of Americans who call themselves African-
Americans?"*
*He: "I think they're crazy—first they call themselves Afro-
Americans now African-Americans. I think they're just
searching for an identity."*
Me: "But why would they need to search for an identity?"
*He: "Because they feel that everyone has a country but they don't,
at least that's what I believe."*
*Me: "But this is their country, so what do you mean they don't
have a country?"*
*He: "Well, you know, other people have a country they can identify
with."*
*Me: "So what's wrong with identifying with America? Black people
in other countries identify themselves with their particular
country. Do you identify yourself with a country other than
America?*
*He: "Not really, I'm American all the way, but my family originally
came from Ireland."*
Me: "Thanks for your time."
He: "My pleasure."

I interviewed many people, most of whom did not care to be called
African-Americans, and still many who did not like hearing the term.
Each person had his or her own view about the *label,* however, after I

shared my point of view, most of them started to see the significance of the interview. Some people were initially apprehensive and were not very cooperative in discussing the topic with me. Maybe because they thought that I was trying to indulge in a dialogue of interracial disharmony; or that the topic did not warrant their interest. The purpose of the interviews, however, was just to glean the proportion of people who were discontented with either hearing or wearing the African-American *label.*

Over a period of years dating back to 1999, I have been asking people the same kinds of questions and giving them my point of view. I remember a graduate student in Philadelphia who became very irate because as far as he is concerned he is not American, but instead African. He was a militant who refused to identify himself with America. He neither considered himself African-American nor American although he was born and raised in America.

There were many people who said that they were not affected one way or another by others using the term *African-American,* because as far as they are concerned they are not African-Americans, and that it did not apply to them. The majority of people in this group were immigrants of Black African descent. Not surprisingly, of course, considering that almost all the immigrants of Black African descent that I have spoken with, do not identify themselves with the term African-American.

In my opinion, many of these people do not look that much different—if at all—form native Black Americans (black people born in America, especially, but not limited to black people born to non-immigrant parents). So why is it that they have such a strong resentment for the term? What I have ascertained from my conversations with people from this group is that, even though these same people have an understanding of their nexus with Africa, they have no desire to conceal their true identity. They want to be identified as who they really are. They have a defined culture and belong to a particular ethnic group that would be obscured by the African-American *label.*

Nobody wants his or her identity to be concealed. Everybody wants to be recognized as part of something—part of a family; part of a group; or a part of a culture, etc. That something, however, has to be genuine. It has to be as solid ground on which one can stand and reach to the sky without worrying about falling; and it has to be unwavering. It is not unlike the wild animals in the jungle. They travel together as a family. They travel together as either herds or flocks. In any one family they are all called by the same name. They are either lions or elephants; or they may be goats or dears, or seagulls. They look out for one another and at times protect one another. They eat together and sometimes even fight among themselves. The bottom line is that they are *called by the same name,* and they are almost impenetrable when they are together. The straggler, however, is the one who strays from the family and is usually devoured.

Though insignificant it may seem, yet I cannot help but believe that we cannot *label* anybody in America with the term *African-American* without deleterious consequences. These consequences, though latent they may seem, I believe will be far more destructive than helpful.

There are many people in America who currently find the term *African-American* repugnant. It is repugnant in one sense because it is like a two-edged sword. On the one side it seems to be all inclusive—espousing all black people in America. On the other side it seems to be segregative—pertaining to only native Black Americans, especially according to the foregoing definition of African-Americans; and also because black immigrants refuse to espouse it.

Therefore, if the term *African-American* is to be a racial description, it would be legitimate only if it would incorporate all black people in America and therefore, all black people in the world, especially since the black population in America is an assortment of people from all over the world, and thus serves as a microcosm. Since that is not possible, then no one should be classified as African-American. It is offensive in another sense because it is very ambiguous in that one can never tell exactly to whom it is being referred, especially when used in the news media.

I find it disgusting when people in the news media use the term African-American to refer to a black person. First of all, it sounds very alien. It seems as if they are talking about someone who is not a legitimate member of the American society—someone who really does not "belong." I would often wonder if black people in American are not insulted to be referred to as if they are foreigners, in their own country.

I know that news journalists are not responsible for coining the term, so there is no blame there. Furthermore, it is difficult to decipher who the term actually represents. *Does it cover everybody who looks black,* or *does it refer to only native Black Americans* (Those born in America especially to non-immigrant parents)? *If the latter is true,* then who can tell the difference between those who are Native Black Americans and those who are not? *If the former is true,* then many people will not be happy because their true identity is actually concealed because *African-American* is not an accurate identification of who they are. How does one delimit the use of the term African-American?

I remember an American television reporter from one of the major networks interviewing one of the Olympic swimmers in the 2004 Olympics in Athens, Greece: She asked the swimmer, "How does it feel to be the first African-American to win a medal in swimming in the Olympics?" As far as I am concerned that was an ambiguous question of which I understood neither its significance nor its relevance. I did not know if the young lady was the first American of black African descent to win a medal, or if she was the first black person in general to win a medal; especially since it appears that many people nowadays are referring to black people in general—especially those who are English-speaking—as African-Americans. Is the ambiguity in this particular example clear to anyone? If the reporter in that particular case was referring to the race of the young lady, then it would indicate that all black people are African-Americans—which is a fallacy because only American people use that term to describe themselves. Surely America is not the world; therefore, it would be presumptuous to define everybody in the world based on America's ideology.

Who really has the right to determine who is, or who is not African-American anyway? I am sure that there are many people in this country who are of mixed races and who do not wish to be *branded* with the term *African-American.* They do not wish to be *labeled* African-American because in so doing they would be suppressing a part of who they are; which could probably be psychologically and emotionally repressive. A typical example is the case in which Tiger Woods refused to identify himself as African-American. I personally agreed with him one hundred percent. What I cannot understand is why so many black people in America have expressed such antagonism toward the man. Why do they want him to say that he is black or African-American or whatever, when his mother is not black or of any African heritage? I am glad that he had the courage to repudiate the claim that he is African-American.

Americans who are half black and half white seem to have always been referred to as African-Americans. Why do they have to be forced into identifying themselves as African-Americans? Is it because "They" say that is what they are? The big "They," of course is the name that black people are apt to use to refer to white people when placing them in a subconsciously superior stratosphere. Or could it be because non-mixed black people do not want these mixed people to think that they are "better than" they are because they are half white? Therefore, they make sure that they tell them who they really are (the so-called African-Americans). Many non-mixed black people tend to display some form of antagonism toward people who are half black and half white because they themselves suffer inferiority complexes due to their ill state of mind.

In particular, are Americans who are half black and half white not just as much of European descent as they are of African descent? So why should they have to succumb to wearing a *label* that others have chosen for themselves; or what others have decided who they are? The days of slavery are long gone and it is time that we worked to overcome its remnants, if that is the real problem.

Of course, we live in a society that requires everyone to be *packaged* properly. However, if we can refer to the people from the island Puerto Rico as Puerto Ricans, most of whom are in the same category of mixed races, then why do we need a label for Americans? Many brown-skinned Puerto Ricans are perhaps more genotypically and phenotypically more black than many half black / half white Americans. Yet, you will never hear them refer to themselves with any African prefix. As far as they are concerned, they are Puerto Ricans. In this day and age one should not be so impassive as to permit others to blindly define who one really is.

Another thing—some Americans do not appreciate the term African-American because it appears to have a negative connotation; as if to say, "Oh you're just an African-American—not a real American." I believe this kind of perception is of the greatest injustice to the great Americans who have sacrificed their lives so that their descendants could become true Americans.

There are also those Americans—naturalized Americans— who do not wish to be referred to as African-Americans. When a black person becomes a naturalized citizen of the United States of America, he or she is told "you are now an American." No one ever says, "You are now an African-American." American, in this particular case is indicating one's nationality—not one's race. Therefore, as far as these people are concerned, they are now Americans by naturalization—a proud moment in their lives. These people, however, still identify themselves with their cultures from their previous countries, and usually have no desire to amalgamate with the African-American ideology which is totally foreign to them.

We have to admit that, when it comes to dealing with racial issues, a lot of us are very confused. Many people do not seem to know how to differentiate between race, ethnicity, culture, and nationality. I often hear people refer to Secretary of State Colin Powell as African-American, but then they refer to Jennifer Lopez as Puerto Rican. They were both born in New York. So how is it that one is African-American and the other Puerto Rican? If her parents are Puerto Ricans and his parents are Jamaicans, then why is he not identified by his ethnic group as she does, instead of being referred to as African-American?

We can clearly see here that the term African-American is being applied as a racial description to classify Colin Powell. For if he were to be classified according to his ethnic group, then he would be an

American of Jamaican descent—not an American-American. Although these ethno-prefixes may be all right in special cases, it is preposterous that only one group in America chooses to be highly conspicuous with the constant "X" prefix identity *label* which does not seem to have a precise meaning.

There is nothing wrong with Jennifer Lopez being identified as a Puerto Rican. The children born in the United States to immigrants from European countries occasionally identify themselves with the country of their parents or fore-parents. That is a way of connecting with their roots, or ancestry. In a casual conversation, for instance, an American of Italian descent often says, "I'm Italian." This of course is not the person's race any more than Puerto Rican is anyone's race; but, this same person of Italian descent—in a different context—will gladly tell you that he or she is American. I have to mention that, I have never heard such a person say that he or she is European-American.

So then, why is it that the children born to black immigrants are dubbed African-Americans? Why are they not identified also with their parents' countries of origin, as other people of non-English-speaking origins? I heard a television reporter say on television, that one of his parents is Puerto Rican; and he referred to himself as Puerto Rican. I have also heard many people refer to him as Puerto Rican even though he was born in New York. So if he can have only one parent be Puerto Rican and he was born in New York and still be considered Puerto Rican, then, how come black people born in America to parents form other countries are dubbed African-Americans? What then is really African-American?

To reiterate the question—are you automatically considered African-American if you are black and American? Can you be diverse like other peoples? By what measure is one considered African-American? If American children born to parents who are not originally from the United States, and are not citizens—which may disqualify these people being African-Americans according to the previous definition—then the family would live in a divided house. The children are called by one name—namely African-Americans—while the parents are called by another name, whatever that may be. This becomes a problem if we are using the term African-American as race. As we mentioned before, one's race is constant. Hence, we cannot have children with one racial identity and parents with a different racial identity if they are technically of the same race. This will tend to lead to isolation, segregation, and confusion of some form.

I often notice too that many people tend to regard "Puerto Rican" as a race. You may have heard people say "Blacks and Puerto Ricans" in a particular context; or you may have heard somebody say "He is not black—he is Puerto Rican." These are examples of common everyday fallacies. How can one say "Blacks and Puerto Ricans" in the same sentence when *Puerto Rican* is not a race? Puerto Rico is a country just as America is a country. In Puerto Rico there are all kinds of people, including black people. The majority of Puerto Ricans are of mixed races, some of which are Black Africans, White Europeans, Indigenous people (Tainos), and others—similar to Dominican people.

The main difference between most Puerto Ricans and most Dominicans, however, is that there are more Dominicans than Puerto Ricans who are mixed with black African ancestry. This is a direct result of the history of the two countries. There were more black slaves imported to the Dominican Republic, and also because of the proximity of the Dominican Republic to Haiti which is predominantly black. Many black Haitians crossed the border into the Dominican Republic and intermingled with the preexisting Dominicans resulting in a nation with far more black people than Puerto Rico. The predominant mixture of races in Puerto Rico is that of the indigenous Tainos and the Spanish settlers. Therefore, Puerto Rico maintains a greater Spanish influence and a greater relative number of people with direct Spanish ancestry. One should understand also that there are black people all over South America and the Caribbean, as mentioned before; and that just because someone speaks Spanish does not mean that he or she is not black, or of black African descent. English is originally from England and Spanish is originally from Spain. So why do so many people still believe that only English-speaking black people are really black?

Incidentally, just because someone's native language is Spanish or some other language other than English does not mean that he or she is not black. In that case most Haitians could say that they are not black—they are Haitians—because they speak French. Language does not define race. Besides, the Caribbean countries and Latin American countries for example, generally consist of people of various races and of mixed races. One of the main differences between the countries in the Caribbean or the Americas, besides the racial mixes, is the language bestowed upon them as a result of conquests. The only reason why people in Puerto Rico, Cuba, Mexico, and most countries in Central and South America speak Spanish is because the Spanish people—from Spain—captured the lands from the original peoples and forced them to speak Spanish. The British, the French and the Dutch did similarly in the countries that today boast the respective languages of their captors. So in reality, all the peoples in these regions who speak Spanish are actually expressing the fact that they are conquered peoples. Yet, so many of these same people celebrate Columbus Day—as if to say, thank you for killing my ancestors.

The language of a particular country in the new world can usually tell a little about the history of that particular country. For example, the British were triumphant over the Spanish in Jamaica, therefore, Jamaicans speak English; the Spanish returned the favor in Puerto Rico, so they speak Spanish, and so on. Therefore, to use *Puerto Rican* and *Black* in the same context is a fallacy of the highest degree; because black people are a race of people whereas *Puerto Rican* is simply designating people from the island of Puerto Rico, some of whom are indeed black, and many of whom are mixed with black.

In like manner, it is a fallacy to say "He is not black, he is Venezuelan" or "She is not black, she is Trinidadian." You could be a black Venezuelan or a black Trinidadian. Black people in other countries, however, do not refer to themselves as African-Americans; and I am quite sure that when they come to America they do not want to be referred to as such.

It appears as if black immigrants who came from countries that are non-Spanish-speaking, are dubbed African-Americans and those from Spanish-speaking countries are dubbed Hispanics or Latinos. As mentioned above, Secretary of State Colin Powell is often referred to as the first African-American to…whatever. However, if he were from a Spanish-speaking country he would probably be dubbed the first Hispanic or Latino to…whatever, even though he is the same person.

A person's race cannot be determined simply by the language that the person speaks. A person born to Chinese parents in Puerto Rico or the Dominican Republic, for example, will naturally grow up speaking Spanish. However, that person is not of Spanish descent because there is no direct bloodline from Spain. In like manner, a person of Spanish descent could be born in a country where Spanish is not the spoken language and therefore grow up not speaking Spanish. So who is the real Hispanic? I once met a Dominican girl who said that her mother is a black Haitian and her father is a white Dutch. Obviously everyone will consider her Hispanic because she is Dominican and she grew up speaking Spanish. However, how different is she from a person born to Chinese parents in a Spanish-speaking country? She definitely does not have any Spanish bloodline. So is she really Hispanic? Is Hispanic a race?

According to the Merriam-Webster Online Dictionary, Hispanic means: *of, relating to, or being a person of Latin American descent living in the U.S.; especially: one of Cuban, Mexican, or Puerto Rican origin.* Of course that includes all other similar peoples. According to this definition anybody without regard to race could be Hispanic, so long as the above criteria are satisfied. Therefore, Hispanic is not a race. To be Hispanic means that you are of Spanish heritage; a result of one's cultural or ethnic influences acquired by birth or association. So a Hispanic person could be black, white, mixed, or other so long as he or she meets the above criteria.

There is also the interchanging use of the terms Latino and Hispanic. It should be understood that Latino is a term reserved only for peoples from Latin American countries, and that Hispanic has a direct correlation with Spain. So a Spanish person living in America is not a Latino. It is more appropriate to refer to that person as either Spanish or Hispanic. Whereas a Latino could be considered Hispanic, a Hispanic does not necessarily have to be Latino. In either case, neither Hispanic nor Latino is disclosing what a person's race is. Sammy Sosa—the famous baseball player—is from the Dominican Republic, which makes him Latino, but he is still a person who is predominantly black. There are also many Latinos who are of white European ancestry, and many others who are of mixed races. Ultimately, one's language does not determine one's race. Not everyone who speaks English is considered a white British person.

The point is not to say that black people in America should not want to identify with their ancestral homeland. I understand absolutely the significance of this grand desire, from the many people that I have spoken with. Yet, if black people in other countries do not seem to have a problem with their identity, meaning that they do not have to remind themselves and others every day that their ancestors are from Africa, why then do we seem to have a problem here in America?

In England a black person does not say "I'm African-British," especially when it is quite obvious what his or her race is. The same goes for a person from Trinidad or Brazil, say. A person from Trinidad, no matter how dominant his African blood, will always say he is Trinidadian—and proud of it. The same goes for a person from Brazil. I have never heard a Jamaican say that he or she is African-Jamaican. The majority of the Jamaican population is of black African descent; and as a people they are very conscious of their African heritage. However, Jamaicans do not identify themselves as "X-Jamaicans." As far as they are concerned, they are Jamaicans.

I was talking with a friend about the African-American terminology when he told me that he had no problem with it since "It is what *they* choose to call themselves," he said. I then told him that as a black man, he himself was not exempted from wearing the *label* when he is out and about in America, which means that it is not just for *them* but for him also. He told me that is not how he defines himself; but I told him that how the general public perceived him was more crucial in this particular perspective than his own perception of himself. We argued back and forth without his gaining any ground on the actual insight of the significance of the conservation. My friend said, "*They* choose to call themselves." The "They" is a separatist term. It indicates that it is fine, so long as I am not included.

One could be liable to think that many problems could arise from such a situation that could result in segregation among American black peoples. Therefore, it should be easy to be believed that the use of the *African-American* terminology to describe people in America is more harmful than helpful. The evidence is in the refusal of every American black person to unequivocally accept the term as a legitimate racial description.

One woman that I interviewed told me that, "Well, we prefer to be called African-Americans because we do not want to be called black." She went on to explain to me the proximity of the word black with the word *Negro* which was used in America in earlier times to refer to black people. She gave me a history of the *name-calling* metamorphosis of black people in America. That same woman, nonetheless, had no problem saying "white people."

So why is it all right to use the term *white people* but not *black people*? How come black people in other countries do not have such a problem? If you wonder why I keep referring to people from other countries, I do so to try to establish uniformity among black people everywhere. From the above discussion I think it is fair to say that since the term African-American cannot be used to classify everybody in America, let alone in the rest of the world, it is therefore, not a proper racial description. It does not include everyone, and furthermore, not everyone wants to be included. Hence it should exclude everyone. For any one people to be considered a race, all must be identified by the same name. Therefore, African-American is not a race.

Chapter 3

Is African-American a Culture?

What constitutes a culture? When we talk about our culture, what are we really talking about? Without regard to race, how can we sometimes identify a particular person with a particular culture? Is the term *African-American* referring to an actual culture? If the term *African-American* is referring to an actual culture, then, who are the actual members of this culture?

When we think of Indian culture, we automatically conjure up in our minds, the way we think people of that culture speak, or dress, or of the delicious foods they eat—or at least what they serve in Indian restaurants throughout the country. Likewise when one thinks of Spanish culture one immediately connects with Flamenco dancing and bull fighting and Spanish art among other things. One can identify British culture with palaces and royalty, the enchanting English accent and of course, the respected educational system. Caribbean culture consists of a myriad of tropical fruits, spicy foods and really *cool laid-back* people. So, with respect to a particular culture, there are attributes that are relatively unique to that culture, that are readily identifiable by others.

I think that just about anyone you ask will be able to give a reasonable definition of what culture is—at least from his or her point of view. Culture constitutes a particular people or group, who share common ideas and customs. The people in a particular culture share common bonds in terms of learned behavioral patterns and beliefs. They generally eat the same kinds of foods and listen to somewhat the same kinds of music, say, and are apt to talk in similar ways.

Sub-cultures within certain cultures may be different from the general or parent culture itself, but can still be identified with that particular culture by someone else outside the culture. The Rasta culture in Jamaica, for example, can normally be identified with Jamaican culture—by someone who is not of Jamaican culture—even though it is a unique culture within the Jamaican culture itself.

There are different sub-cultures within Indian culture separated not only by language, but also by class and the cast system, among other things. Nonetheless, anyone outside Indian culture can usually identify a particular person with that culture, regardless of the person's variance within the culture. So the relative uniqueness of a particular culture makes it identifiable by others. The relative uniqueness of a culture is the common denominator that serves as the attractive force for all its members.

That culture is like an attractive force that keeps people bound to a common ground, is why nobody wants to be misidentified. Most people enjoy a sense of belonging to their particular cultures. When they are with people of their own culture they communicate better and they feel right at home. Cultural identity is very important to most people because they are proud of their culture and it serves as a platform for them to show the world who they are, and who or what they represent. Sometimes some cultural groups demonstrate ostentatiously—especially during the summertime—their cultural attributes at the different state fairs and festivals across the United States. They want to show the world how special their culture is, and hope that others will come to appreciate their culture by participating in their festivities.

It is quite clear that one's culture is a vital part of one's well-being. We use our culture as a way to identify ourselves and we need our culture to connect with our common history. Our culture needs us to propagate its spirit, so to speak, to future generations.

Is there an American culture that can categorically embrace all Americans indiscriminately? America is a multicultural society, which makes it difficult to classify all Americans as members of the same culture. That is, America is not only racially divided, but culturally divided as well. There are cultures and sub-cultures in New York that are quite different form cultures and sub-cultures in Texas, for example.

Particular ethnic groups are more inclined to have prominent cultures that are readily identifiable by the general population; whereas a typical culture among those considered non-ethnic can sometimes be obscure. I have often heard that southern culture is the real American culture. Maybe it is viewed that way because of traditional things that everyone in the world can identify the south with—things such as country music, southern foods, and country lifestyle.

Although non-immigrant black and white Americans in most cases share night and day cultural experiences, either can usually be identified as Americans by many people outside the United States—especially by speech patterns if not by anything else. However, culture is not mere language—it is a lifestyle.

As we have already mentioned, America cannot be defined by one culture, but let us take it a step further—are all white Americans of the same culture? I think we all know the answer to that question is no! White Americans come from varying backgrounds based on their European ancestral heritage. The cultural differences among white Americans vary in much the same way as non-white cultural groups. Irish-Americans celebrate their cultural heritage as do Italian-Americans, Polish-Americans, Russian-Americans and others such as the Greek-Americans and German-Americans.

The so-called non-ethnic white Americans may not be as conspicuous culturally, because they are generally far removed from their European ancestral heritage. Consequently they tend not to display a cultural heritage—which is why they are perceived as bland by some cultural groups. The point is that we do not see all white Americans as the same people. We differentiate among white Americans as descendants of Italian, Irish, Russian, German and Polish, for example. We see them as people from different cultural backgrounds.

If we can come to the conclusion that white Americans are categorically different, culturally, then what about black Americans—

are they culturally different too? Or does America view all black people as one people, with no cultural distinction? Considering this, the question is: Is the term *African-American* a cultural term? Is it a term that categorizes American people according to culture? If it is a cultural term, then, does it imply that if you are black in America, then you are automatically of *African-American* culture? If not, then how can it be used as liberally as it is without causing confusion and resentment among the different cultural black groups—and not to mention among the general population?

Let us assume that the term *African-American* is a cultural term. How would one define *African-American* culture? Would such a culture embody all black people in America? Or would it espouse only native black Americans? If only non-immigrant black Americans are considered, then can we reasonably say that all such people share the commonalities that are assigned to the paradigm of a true culture? If *African-American* culture constitutes all black people in America, does it mean that there is no cultural diversity among black American people?

Furthermore, what about black people born and raised in American households to immigrants who keep their traditions from their country of origin; and who might not share much in common with native black people? Surely these black people would not really satisfy the African-American cultural paradigm if there is one, because the elements of comparison between the two groups would be obviously different.

Let us consider native black people who can trace their roots as far back as they can such that, as far as they know, they are not descendants of recent immigrants. So, as far as *African-American culture* is concerned, it should theoretically incorporate or embody all such people—one would think. Even though there are cultural differences among native black people from north to south and from east to west across the United States, it is quite easy for some people to identify them as Americans regardless of where in the world they are. How can one tell that they are Americans and not Africans or English, although they could look very much like people from Africa or England? Many people can tell right away that they are Americans. Why?

Black people in New York have a very different culture from black people in Texas or Louisiana, say. These people are different in many ways: dialect, food, music, art, mannerism, among other things. Therefore, let us see if we can conclude that *African-American* is really a cultural term.

The fact that these people—whether they are from New York or Texas—can be identified by just about anyone anywhere as Americans, means that there is something unique about them that sets them apart. It does not matter if they look like Africans; people can tell that they are Americans. That is very important to most people—to be recognized as who one really is. The real problem here, though, is identifying these people with perceptible cultural differences as people of *African-American culture.* The problem is exacerbated when we try to include immigrant black people and those Americans born to immigrant black people. Where is the demarcation for who is, and who is not African-American?

If African-American is a cultural term with a requirement that to be African-American, one has to be born in America, then it becomes more preposterous when one considers Americans born to immigrant parents. It should be quite clear to most people that Americans born to immigrants of black African descent are more likely to be raised in a very different cultural environment and hence apt to have different cultural characteristics form those of native black Americans. Furthermore, when we consider the naturalized Americans who came from all over the world along with their cultures, and the children born to these people, it is obviously impossible to demarcate a specific African-American culture based on physical appearance as used by the general public.

From a media perspective, it appears that all black people in America are dubbed African-Americans regardless of who they are and without reservation. The fact is, black people here are as culturally diverse as the fishes of the ocean. Therefore, the African-American terminology as currently used is not an acceptable cultural indicator for American black peoples.

If a police officer stops a man walking down the street and calls in on his radio and describes the man as an African-American male; but it turns out the man is actually Ethiopian, maybe not even an American citizen: would that be a true description of the man? Even if the man were a naturalized American citizen or a born American to Ethiopian immigrants, would it make a difference in who he really is? Culturally, he would be perceived as someone who is part of the class but who is not enrolled. It is more likely that this man did not tell anyone that he is African-American or identified himself with the term. Nevertheless, he would be involuntarily and inappropriately misidentified.

Personally, I believe that it is downright ludicrous for American people to involuntarily assume an identity whether cultural, racial or otherwise, placed on them by some unknown entity. It is even more irritating that Americans are forced to use this separatist and repugnant identity whether overtly or covertly, and not to mention, so impassively like a lamb going to the slaughter without questioning its long-term ramifications.

If the term African-American is being used as a cultural identification that is supposed to be an actual representation of all Americans who are black, then it would be a misleading notion and would serve only to diminish the power of black people in America. We have to come to the point of appreciation of the different cultures among American black people, in the same manner that we can appreciate the different cultural groups among other Americans, such as Americans of European descent.

Yet, Americans of European descent do not identify themselves everyday as *X-Americans*. They are quite sure of themselves—they know who they are. With that said, do black American people know who they are? Is there an identity problem among the black American population? To say that someone is the first African-American to win a medal in the Olympics: Would that be a true comprehensible statement? Not to me. I would not be able to tell if it is the first black person in general, or if it is the first black American person, considering the general use of the term these days.

The term African-American could be used as a cultural term if and only if there was a clear picture of exactly who belongs to such a culture—not when every black person in America is being referred to as African-American. To be of Italian culture, one has to be of Italian heritage, not of European heritage in general. Black people that constitute the American population are all of different cultural heritages, not unlike the countries in the continent of Africa. Therefore, as a people, we can all be Americans, accepting our cultural differences and celebrating our oneness, so that we can identify with other black people throughout the world without any ambiguities.

Chapter 4

Is African-American an Ethnic Group?

When one thinks of an ethnic group one usually thinks of a group of people sharing many things in common which does not necessarily include the color of one's skin. People of the same ethnic group generally share cultural characteristics such as language, mannerism, diet, and sometimes physical appearance among other things. The *Webster's New World College Dictionary* (Fourth Edition), defines Ethnic as: *Designating or of a population subgroup having a common cultural heritage or nationality, as distinguished by customs, characteristics, language, common history, etc.* This same dictionary defines African-American as *black American.*

Therefore, the question of interest here is: Can all black people in America be classified as ethnically the same and therefore be grouped as African-Americans?

From the above definition, it is clear to see that *African-American* is definitely not an ethnic group because there are many black American people who do not share anything in common besides skin color. Native black Americans and naturalized black Americans are very different in almost every respect. Naturalized black Americans and Americans born to black immigrants, apt to have customs, characteristics, common history, and sometimes language that are conspicuously different from native black Americans.

Even among the different immigrant groups, there are ethnic differences. Black Americans who are raised in a Nigerian household do not have much in common with Americans raised in an Ethiopian household. The same goes for black Americans raised in a Dominican household or a Jamaican household, say. This takes us back to the question once again about the distinguished Collin Powell. Why is he identified as African-American? Is African-American his race or his ethnic group? Since we have already established that African-American is not a race, then it is evident that it cannot be his race. So then, why is he not identified by his ethnic group? The answer to that, however, is that there seems to be no established Jamaican ethnic group as there is a Puerto Rican ethnic group.

Based on the common use of the term African-American, one would be inclined to believe that General Powell did not tell anyone that he is African-American anyway; but as many Americans are involuntarily *labeled* with this insidious title, he too is a victim. Of course, his powerful image may not be diminished by the absurd title, but why should he be called an African-American when his peers of European descent are called Americans?

Americans should eradicate this African-Americanism and assume their true titles as Americans. Besides, it could be that only a proportionally small number of Americans have assumed this title and of course indoctrinated many other legitimate Americans to do the same. Americans should not be so gullible, especially when it is a matter of national pride and self-respect. Many Americans of time past fought against all kinds of adversities to procure American citizenship for themselves and their descendants; now their descendants retroactively call their fore-parents African-Americans. Whose idea was it anyway—that legitimate Americans need an "X" identity *label?* Why would so many intelligent Americans be so willing to surrender to such absurdity?

We have established that all black people in America cannot be grouped together as one ethnic group because of the great diversity among black American peoples. Furthermore, we have established that African-American cannot be an ethnic group, especially because there can be no clear demarcation for such a group. As far as the media is concerned, can anyone really tell who is African-American and who is not? Should a demarcation be recognized, and if so how would it be implemented? Can anyone tell which American is of German descent and which is of French descent? Likewise, it is not always easy to tell which American is of Chinese descent and which is of Japanese descent except for the difference in names. The point here is that the term African-American is not a legitimate term for an ethnic group—it is a fabricated term that has many people confused—and no American should be considered as belonging to an ethnic group that he or she did not choose as his or her own.

As far as I know, members of particular ethnic groups are usually highly offended whenever they are misidentified. For example, an American who is ethnically Chinese does not want to be identified as ethnically Japanese. Likewise, an American who is ethnically Italian will not like it very much if he is identified as ethnically Polish and visa versa. So, by the same argument, why should all black American people be identified as belonging to the same ethnic group, if indeed the African-American term is effecting such an emotion? Consequently, since most of the people who are being identified as African-Americans did not choose the term as their own (from my personal interviews), it proves therefore to be a tool of misidentification. It is a term that is forced on American people which is inappropriate, offensive and illegal.

Chapter 5

Is African-American a Nationality?

According to *The American Heritage Dictionary of the English Language* - Fourth Edition, nationality is the status of belonging to a particular nation by origin, birth, or naturalization. The section for Nationality in the American passport is filled in as United States OF America. However, the colloquial expression for the nationality of a citizen of the United States of America, is American.

Although Canadians are actually North Americans and people from the South American continent are also technically Americans, people generally think of United States citizens only, as Americans. How many people ever really think of Guyanese as Americans? I personally have never heard anyone refer to Canadians as Americans, at least not in the U.S. Ultimately, as far as most people are concerned, Americans are citizens of the United States of America; and *American* is what United States citizens accept as their nationality.

As far as nationality is concerned—to reiterate—it is usually identified with the country of which one is a citizen. Therefore, when one is asked one's nationality, one usually replies by giving the name of the country of which one is a citizen. Hence, the nationality of a Brazilian citizen is Brazilian. Additionally, nationality is invariable— all citizens of the same country share the same nationality, which is identified by a unique name. No one can mistake a German national for a Chinese national—the names are not unique. So then, can all American citizens be identified as African-Americans, as their nationalities? The answer to this question should be quite obvious.

If African-American is a nationality, then, all Americans would have to be called African-Americans because all citizens of the same country share the same nationality; but we all know that this is absolutely absurd. Can you imagine the president being addressed as African-American President Bush? That in itself sounds laughable.

Why would any American want to be identified as anything but American? As a heterogeneous society, Americans are racially diverse, but all are Americans, nonetheless. The relative harmonious racial diversity of American cities is what makes America one of the most unique countries in the world. Americans seem to be able to tolerate one another's racial differences without any uprising.

However, when black American people assume an obscure identity that in effect makes them contemptuously conspicuous; and which could probably isolate them from the rest of the population, the result can only be one of total destruction of future growth as a people. Why should any American choose to be called African-American? If someone asks you your nationally, what will your reply be? Will it be American or African-American? Certainly it cannot be African-American because there is no such nationally—there is no country by the name African-America.

A friend of mine identifies himself as American of Chinese descent. This makes more sense to me. He was born in America and most people could probably guess that he is of Chinese descent. The important thing is that he identifies himself as American; and regardless of his race, that is what he is.

I can certainly say that normally I do not hear Americans who are of Chinese descent—whether on television or on radio— posing as Chinese-Americans. They normally identify themselves as Americans, and only if needed they will disclose their ethnicity; and it is usually not in the form of X-American.

The issue of African-Americanism may not seem to be of any importance to many black American people, but the resultant effects can be tremendous with time. Americans should identify themselves as Americans. If you carry an American passport, you are an American. Your ethnicity is of subsequent importance. However, the current issue here is to show that African-American is not a nationality.

In addition to some of the things that we have mentioned, one thing should be clear; and that is: in order for one's nationality to be African-American, one will have to be from a country called African-America. Since there is no such country, there can be no such nationality. Also because not all Americans can categorically be identified as African-Americans— which is the criterion for the American nationality—we can say with much confidence that African-American is not a nationality.

Chapter 6

Latent Effects of African-Americanism

Could there be an emotional or a psychological impediment in referring to, as African-Americans, American people who are of black African descent? If so, could this impediment abate American black people's natural progression up the American economic, social and educational ladder? Does the African-American terminology connote second-class citizenship or foreigner? These are some of the consequential implications that we could debate. Also if one thinks of the political implications of misrepresentation due to improper identification, then it is easy to see one of the actual ramifications of using the term African-American as a descriptive (racial, cultural, ethnic or national) indicator.

The actual psychological or emotional effect of the use of the *African-American* terminology as a labeling tool—for what appears to be all black people in America—is not easy to procure. It may seem as though everything is all right. Everyone is going about his or her day-to-day business and living by the rule of political correctness. There seems to be no problem at all. Yet, has anyone ever stop to think of how he or she, as a black person living in America, is perceived by the general population? We often hear that we are perceived according to the image we project; and that perception is reality. Some American black people among themselves may not think that there is a real problem because they themselves do not have an actual problem with the terminology. Those who are proponents of the *title* of African-American may say that they want to identify with the content of Africa. That is fine! I personally have no problem with that.

However, citizens of other countries normally identify themselves as nationals of the country in which they were born and raised. That gives them a feeling of belonging and a sense of national pride. A person from Germany will say "I'm German." So, if as an American you identify yourself as African-American, what kind image are you projecting and how are you perceived by Americans of other races? Do you have a feeling of nationalism?

If one was born and raised in this country, then one is an American. As an American, one is entitled to all the rights and privileges of an American citizen. If one relinquishes one's rights as a citizen by proclaiming that one is not American even though one was born here, or has been naturalized, then one should accept the consequences of disassociation or repudiation. I am referring to black American people who continue to view themselves as inferior subjects, and who continue to believe that black American people are not really Americans—and believe me—I have spoken with many of these Americans. I do believe that those black Americans, who vehemently deny their status as Americans, should be charged with high treason. Their reprehensible act of repudiation of the legacy of all kinds of freedom bestowed upon them by their predecessors should be considered in the highest court of racial equality and equal justice. Those are the legacies for which their predecessors shed their blood, and many others made great sacrifices to effect change in this country. Therefore, it should be a reprehensible act for this generation to disregard its legacy and to discontinue the struggle for justice and equal treatment for black Americans and all American peoples.

If an American does not feel as though he is a veritable citizen, then it is obvious that he cannot develop a sense of belonging or a sense of national pride. He will therefore, continue to walk along the path of maladjustment and despair, and will never be able to *pull his head out of the sand,* so to speak. Shame and subserviency will forever be his clothing; and false pride and disunity with his neighbor will be his diversion.

When a young black American child has to grow up wearing a *label* every day, especially when his white American peers do not have to do the same; how will he thrive consciously and subconsciously? Will he develop feelings of inferiority complexes which may be due to an identity that is perceived as an outsider? Will he ever aspire to be the employer instead of the employee? Or will he think that only veritable Americans can be employers, and he is just an African-American? Furthermore, how can two children be born and raised in America, one called American and the other African-American, without there being some kind of pernicious shortcoming, whether subconscious or otherwise? If we can come to the point of appreciating and celebrating the differences of the peoples of our society, then there is no need to constantly bring these differences to the forefront. We are *one nation under God,* represented by peoples of all kinds, including American black people.

The reason why it is so important to be called Americans and not African-Americans, is a matter of self-respect and respect for all the people who shed their blood and made great sacrifices, so that black people in America could attain the right to be recognized as true Americans.

When a white customer walks into a restaurant anywhere in America, without any other information other than his appearance, one presumes only one thing—he is an American customer. No one is going to say, "Here comes a European-American customer." This customer is not known to wear a *label* of any kind other than the *American* one. Naturally he will be treated as a legitimate American. A black American citizen deserves the right to experience all the rights and privileges the same as a white American citizen under the law. Therefore, he or she should expect the same treatment; as of any human being for that matter.

However, without considering the law, black American people need to think of themselves as legitimate Americans without the need for a *label.* When you tell me that you are an African-American, the first thing that comes to mind is that you do not view yourself as a true American, but as someone who is unsure of his status in his own land. Of course, that may not be how you think of yourself, but that is the way

I perceive you; which means that others are likely to perceive you the same way too—*that is the image you project.*

If I thought that someone was referring to me as African-American, I would have been looking behind me to see who was there; because I definitely would not have responded. If it were certain that it was me to whom the person was trying to communicate. I would probably have responded by saying, "Sorry! But I'm no darn African-American, I'm American!" I definitely think that the term African-American is an outright disrespectful and diminishing tool, and serves no advantageous purpose whatsoever.

If an American black male is treated with less than acceptable manners or treated with disrespect, so to speak, by white restaurant attendants, say; it could be because he is automatically perceived as different, especially due to the prominent alien *label* that he is donning. Or it could be just due to uninitiated attendants in customer service. It is hard to tell, but donning the African-American *label* which probably connotes alien status does not help. The customer naturally will become emotional about the unfair treatment and perhaps will assume that it is the result of him being "African-American." However, what would the scenario be if he adorns himself as a legitimate American and demands the same respect as other Americans—not unlike his white compatriots?

Maybe the outcome would be different now that he is perceived differently by others; and maybe he himself would have a different view of his position as an American. In American society, foreigners of non-white racial groups are normally treated with less respect than foreigners of white European descent. Consequently, when one assumes the title of *African-American* it could result in further perpetuation of the alien status originally assigned to American black folks who were considered no more than three-fifths of a person, let alone a true American.

Dr. Martin Luther King led the Civil Rights Movements that culminated ultimately in black American people being recognized as legitimate citizens with the right to vote. Since then as a people, black Americans, including naturalized Americans, have made great strides toward equality. However, we have come to a point in America where it seems as if we are trying to turn the gold back into straw.

One deleterious effect that could result from African-Americanism is misrepresentation in numbers of American black people. This could be true, because many naturalized Americans that I have spoken with, said they normally put *other* as their racial identity whenever they fill out a form. They said that they will not identify themselves as African-Americans, because as far as they are concerned, it is not a true representation of who they are. It is an identity with which they have no nexus. Therefore, if one tries to make a head count of Americans who are actually of black African descent, one will come up short if one is counting only the indicated so-called "African-Americans."

I believe that it is imperative that black American people decide whether or not they are indeed true Americans, just the same as white Americans believe that they are true Americans. In so doing, black American people can come to the crossroad of ultimate decision—do they have roots planted or transplanted in American soil? This is absolutely necessary for exponential growth as a people in America, whether psychologically, educationally, socially or economically. The fact is American black people do have deep roots in American soil, a fact they need to accept and cherish.

I do not think that very many people like a garden with only one kind of flower or a garden with flowers of only one color. Therefore, we have to appreciate our garden the way it is. We are all blessed to be part of the beautiful garden along with all the other flowers. The master of the garden sprinkles on us the same amount of water as the other flowers. Some of us need the special touch of the master's hand to help us grow in the right direction; some of us just need to know that there are others around us who care for us and want to see us grow and blossom into magnificent adults.

It is hard for us to effectively care for one another if we are too busy worrying about spreading our leaves as wide as we possibly can to catch the most sun; while there are some deep in the shadows gasping for a little sunlight. Getting too much sun can be just as dangerous as not getting any sun at all; so watch out! One thing is certain, the master makes sure that we are all given enough water to survive and the soil here is rich; so it is our responsibility to make sure that we are not blocking anyone's sunlight, thus, preventing his or her growth. Furthermore, we should try to clear a sunlit path so others can thrive.

Individual achievement and cultural differences among black American people should be embraced by all black people living in America; however they should not repress or forestall the general progression and growth of the people as a whole. As far as empowerment of black people is concerned, it is not about who can drive the finest car, or who can live in the grandest house or who has the most education; and it is definitely not about who has the most money. Regardless of who you may think you are, as a black person living in America, you will always be judged by the general perception of black people in America; and that perception is not just by non-black people, but naturally by fellow black people as well.

Black people love to decry racial intolerance by people of other races (specifically, Americans of European descent), but fail to acknowledge that they themselves are, at times, as brutal as or even more so, toward their own kind than people of other races. Black people tend to give Americans of European descent more respect than they do their own kind; but the reverse is almost never true. Therefore, until we as a people shed the coating of self-hatred, and learn to respect and care for one another, and be our brother's and sister's keepers, whether we like one another or not, we will never gain the respect of other peoples, or of one another for that matter.

Yes, there are malignant members of the family who we would love to reject; but all families have those members. Therefore, if we can help some to realize their potentials and climb closer to their dreams, then all kinds of growth could be in perpetual motion. As it is in military training—if one member fails then everybody fails—American black people need to stop looking at the individual achievement of the few and focus on the achievement of the whole.

Black American people—regardless of culture or ethnicity—have to work to empower one another for the general progression of the whole. That is a responsibility that lies among the people and should not be expected to come from outside. As a people we are judged as the whole and not as individuals. There is nothing wrong with that, because that is how everyone else is judged every day; and black people themselves tend to judge people of other races the same way too. That is why one can often hear black people talking about how smart Asian people are. Black people generally judge Asian people as a group. They tend to think that all Asian people know Kung Fu or Karate; or that they are all smart in everything. Of course, those of us who are enlightened know better.

Native black Americans should stop seeing immigrant black Americans as different kinds of people. Do not forget that German prisoners could go to places where legitimate American black soldiers were not permitted. The point is that white Americans do not care where other white people come from—all they care about is that they are white. Therefore, black American people should adopt the same principle. All black American people should be identified as legitimate Americans, whether they are native or naturalized; and black people in general should be viewed as one people, or as people of the same race, while accepting cultural and ethnic differences.

Now that we have established that the term *African-American* does not represent a race, a culture, a nationality or an ethnic group, and since there are many people who apparently are offended by it; it obviously should no longer be ascribed to veritable American people. Its discontinued use will undoubtedly minimize any clandestine harmful psychological, emotional, or social effects, or eliminate any feelings of inferiority. Finally, Americans should address themselves as Americans without any "X" prefix. Nonetheless, it may be deemed appropriate to say an American black male or an American white male where necessary; but not one American and the other African-American. Such inconsistency is bound to lead to social inequality in addition to other inequalities, whether overt or covert.

Chapter 7

Let's Talk About Race Relations in America

As Americans, we should have a duty of service to our country and to our fellow people. We are indeed our brother's keeper. In order for us to continue to have a great America, we have to have great Americans. We have to work as a people united to continue to build America, and not as a people divided with a concomitant degradation of the American will. We have to try to inculcate the premise that we have to care for one another as a united people; in spite of the differences in race, culture, ethnicity or any other factor. We also need to embrace the principle that an evil act against an American is an evil act against America. Americans are the elemental structures of the compound unit of America. A severe damage to any internal elemental structure can result in collapse of the whole compound unit. Such destruction can probably be more easily conceived than any external bombarding forces.

Regardless of race, ethnicity, creed, or gender, all Americans should have access to basic resources— resources that will enable or empower them to be more valuable to their community, and to the American society as a whole. Lacking resources necessary for intellectual and social growth can lead to the decay of these necessary building fabrics. Such decay can ultimately result in antagonistic relations, especially between white and black peoples. Maybe, the disproportionate acquisition of resources between the two groups (with black people obviously being the disenfranchised of the two), has caused many Americans to develop complexes of inferiority, manifesting in social subservient behaviors. The depravation of black people in America seems to have caused much discontentment among the common people, resulting in social antagonisms directed toward fellow black people, as well as toward fellow white Americans. The inferiority complexes mentioned above could have arisen as a result of the predominant and persistent subservient positions that black American people endure. Continuous depravation and enervating hope can lead to despair and antagonistic social relationships.

Although not usually obvious to those unable to discern it, there seems to be a very serious case of enmity between white and black Americans. On the surface things can appear to be all right; white people and black people working together and seem to have amiable relationships in most cases; but beneath the surface it is easy to discern much enmity between the common people. This enmity is mostly unilateral—radiating from white to black. The black recipient at times tries to reflect the radiation back to its source, but the reflecting surface is very poor. Therefore, the radiation does not always return to, or reach its original source. Hence the enmity radiating from white Americans has a more profound effect on black Americans than does the converse. Why this continuous and undying enmity in our "One nation under God?" Let us explore the possible causes and later try to find solutions.

It is easy to believe that the antagonistic social relationship between white people and black people in America started with the onset of slavery. Black slaves in America were recognized as subjects less than humans. As a result, white people in America assumed the superior position while subjecting black people to the inferior position. Since then these etched positions have not been actually eradicated. The Emancipation Proclamation deemed black slaves free. However, when the slaves were proclaimed free, what were they actually freed from? The obvious answer would be that they were freed from forced labor; but were these people really free indeed? Certainly they were no longer shackled, but were they able to reconcile themselves to the impetuous change from bondage to freedom? Or perhaps they had become zombie-like, unable to recapture their lost souls; resulting in their precarious journey in the abyss of despair and bittersweet freedom.

On the other hand, were white slave masters conceptually receptive to the actual freedom of the slaves; or did they still consider them slaves—permanently—for as long as they shall live? The Emancipation Proclamation might have freed the slaves from forced labor, but it surely did not heal the scars of years of psychological and emotional devastation. Emancipation was the dawning of a new relationship between the former slave and former slave master. That is where antagonism and hatred theoretically evolved in the new relationship. In that new relationship, the former slave and former slave master were now co-existing and intermingling—an atmosphere that the former slave master totally repudiated. Therefore, he enacted antagonism toward the former slave resulting in what is called racism. That is where the enmity developed and has transcended the generations.

To digress: As far as the relationship between slave and slave master was concerned, my theory is that slavery abated the courage of its victims and almost completely destroyed their innate human spirit. The tenet of slavery had wounded its victims so profoundly, that some of the wounds were never healed—they were left open or exposed, and have probably become sores today. Perhaps those open or exposed wounds could not find the right conditions to heal themselves. The healing process requires favorable conditions without which the wound could take a long time to heal or not heal at all. Healing follows a cascade of events, which was not initiated after the emancipation event. Instead, the former slave master perpetuated his preponderance of power over the former slave—a condition unfavorable for healing in that particular case. Incidentally, perhaps only the Master Physician can mend those wounds—an avenue to consider if needed.

One could theorize that many of the former slaves remained slaves though not enslaved. Therefore, no physical shackles were needed because they were already raped of their humanity and were willing to accept with alacrity, any inferior position in the "white man's" world. That is probably why so many black people today still maintain an inferior disposition in what they believe to be the "white man's" world. How is it possible for someone to be a slave without being enslaved? A good analogy is that of a prostitute and her client. The client may buy her services for a particular time period; but he can never buy her heart—that she has to give willingly. That same prostitute will pass her former client on the street when she is not working, and just ignore him if he tries to talk to her. In like manner, it should be easy to understand that one can be enslaved without actually being a slave. For one to be a slave, one would have to succumb to the will of the enslaver emotionally, spiritually, socially, and psychologically. In other words, one would have to surrender one's will. Ultimately, the choice would be that of the enslaved to decide whether or not he is willing to surrender his entire human spirit and become someone's slave; whether he is in shackles or not. That is to say, he could choose to be an incorrigible slave such that, as soon as the shackles are removed he would revert to his former self, or he could choose to continue under the spell of the enchanter.

If one is able to revert to one's former self after enslavement, then what that would mean is that one would not continue under the spell of the "white man." Therefore, one would not be led to believe that one is inferior to another. In effect, those black people who continue to walk in their perpetual trance of inferiority would be able to snap out of their trance and experience a new birth of true liberty. My philosophy is that true freedom can never be bought—it is a state of mind. Unfortunately, not many slaves were able to retain their inner light after the shackles were removed; so they continued to look to the "white man" to provide their light and to be their guide—a behavior that has continued to this day.

Slavery had broken the spirits of its victims such that they subsequently became sequacious subjects to their master. They were eager to please the master not unlike the master's own pet dog. Incidentally, they were treated worse than the master's pet dog, and as a consequence, many of these slaves developed a condition that I consider to be the *puppy dog mentality syndrome* or PDMS. As far as the master's pet dog is concerned, it will always respond to the master's beck and call. All that the master has to do is give the dog a little attention—pat it on its head and throw it a bone every now and then, and the dog will wag its tail and show reverence to its master. PDMS is a servile state of mind that is either imposed on, or voluntarily assumed by its victims. The victims are usually in a state such that they are always trying to ingratiate themselves with whoever is in the superior position. While trying to be on the Master's "good side," so to speak, or trying to win his favor, the PDMS victim will normally reject his colleagues. There are two forms of PDMS: (1) Imposed PDMS and (2) Assumed PDMS. (1) Imposed PDMS—The Master inflicts it by giving one or more subordinates special attention, or at least makes them feel as if they are more in his favor than the others; (2) Assumed PDMS—It is manifested when an underling or subordinate craves the attention of the Master, while pretending to be superior to his or her colleagues. The victim of either form of PDMS lives under the false impression that his association with the master makes him superior to those of his kind or associates.

The slave master was probably well aware that he could have harnessed any needed power by inflicting PDMS on some of the slaves. Was he really smart enough to dissemble his motives when he gave some slaves special treatment, knowing that they would have developed PDMS? Or did it just happen by chance? In any case this condition caused disunity among the slaves because those in the Master's favor repudiated their own kind to secure their favored positions. That dissension between the Favored and the Rest was a powerful tool that the Master wielded. The slave who suffered form PDMS served only the Master and himself. He would have cut the throat of any other slave who rose up against the Master.

PDMS existed then, and it has transcended the generations to today's generation. There are many black people in today's society who demonstrate this insidious condition. It is prevalent in the classroom, in the workplace, in the church—in fact it is common in every facet of society. It is common everywhere where black people are subjugated to white people; it is even common in other countries where white people are in the minority. All that the so-called "white man" has to do is give a black man a little attention and he (the black man) is bought. He will have become the wagging-tail puppy dog who will destroy any other dog that comes nigh his master.

PDMS is a common occurrence in American society, and elsewhere too. However, we shall focus on PDMS in America. It was a condition that kept the slaves divided, and still serves as a major divider among black people today. In the classroom, for example, PDMS can manifest itself through a host black student who claims that all his friends are white and so he cannot relate to black people. Or because he grew up in a white neighborhood he can relate only to white people. This is probably the kind of student that some black students consider "acting white." PDMS is a very serious condition that can lead its victims along a slippery path of maladjustment. If it is not identified and treated, a particular victim will probably never find true contentment because of disharmony with himself.

On the contrary, from what I have observed, no matter how much a white person "hangs out" with black people, he is always able to relate to his own kind. I have not yet seen a situation where a white American disassociates himself from, or rejects other white Americans just because he has black friends. As a matter of fact, black people are the only ones whom I have observed thus far in America, to display such behavior of hatred-of-own-kind and disunity. Could it be that there are still open wounds that need special care in order to heal? If one considers the above scenario with the black student who claims that he cannot relate to black people: his white friends are relating to him and he is black. So how come he himself cannot relate to other black people? The truth is: he is suffering from PDMS. This hatred that black people have developed for one another that has transcended the generations, needs immediate attention. A starting point is to focus on healing the wounds, so that they can at least develop scabs and become well and rid the body of any further pain. Do not forget that the wounds require proper medicine and favorable conditions.

Before we talk about the required medicine and the favorable conditions, let us talk some more about PDMS. Any black person in America who has ever worked in an environment where almost everybody is white, with a few sprinkles of black people, must have been exposed to PDMS of some form. You could be the new black person on the job where already existed another black person, who refuses to acknowledge you even though all the white people on the job welcome you with open arms, and display their excellent social skills. The PDMS victim seems to think that if he interacts with you, he will lose his social standing with his white co-workers, who ironically are interacting with you. It usually turns out that he is the only person on the job who does not talk with you. PDMS is more evident in predominantly white environments where the "black man," regardless of social status in most cases, craves the friendship and approval of the "white man." He tends not to associate with people of his kind; and if you—a black man—are sitting in one corner of the room, he will sit in the opposite corner as far away from you as possible. PDMS is a very serious destructive device that creates only victims.

I once asked a graduate student in Philadelphia the following questions: Why do black students always seem to avoid sitting close to one another in the big classrooms (auditoriums)? Why do they seem to avoid interacting with one another—if one is sitting on one side of the room, the other will almost always deliberately sit on the opposite side of the room? He replied by saying: "Man, I'm glad you ask that question because it's something I used to do all the time; but I never knew why I did it—I just used to do it subconsciously." He continued to say, "Since I became a Muslim, I don't do it anymore, but sometimes I catch myself tending to do it." Those questions were appropriate because it was easy to see that students of other races, such as Asian students, for instance, always tried to find one another and sat close together; and white students undoubtedly clustered. Only black students were usually separated.

The American classroom is, to some extent, a microcosm of American society; with black people as usual being the only unconsolidated group. I am sure we can all agree that as a nation we have to think cohesively. However, black people should not try to integrate with others just because they despise their own kind. It is time that black people developed a sense of racial pride and find the beauty and strength in themselves, independent of what others think of them. Black people have to create their own attractive world that will be attractive to others; so that others will be the ones who would like to come in; instead of black people forcing themselves into other peoples' antagonistic world where they are not welcomed. Black people have to change their positions such that they become the host instead of being the guests all the time. We need to host the party instead of going to the party. If they do not want us to drink from their water fountains, then we have to build our own water fountains.

I have not observed to any significant degree, the overt tension and disunity displayed by black people, in any other racial group. Asian people will almost always find other Asian people, no matter how huge the crowd. Even though I must admit, that there is a very small number of non-traditional Asians who display symptoms of PDMS. These are the Asians who apparently find beauty only in white people. Everything they do is centered on their relationships with white people. You never see them with other Asian people. I once had a roommate who is completely Chinese—both his parents are from China—who told me that his parents are Chinese but he his white. This guy was not joking at all—he was dead serious. He even avoided eating rice because he did not want to associate himself with the stereotype of Chinese and rice. He also said that he had been eating rice from he was a child, and that he hated it. I told him that I had been eating rice from I was a child too, and that I still did and loved it.

I once worked at a pharmaceutical company whereby just about everybody in my environment was white. I remember clearly one Indian girl and a Mexican. I tried talking Spanish with the Mexican guy, when told me that he did not speak Spanish. He said that he grew up in Texas and that he never learned Spanish. I immediately thought to myself: Wow, another PDMS victim. I thought that maybe he refused to speak Spanish because he wanted to assimilate into the white environment and remain inconspicuous. There is nothing wrong with that if it were possible, and if he could avoid losing himself. However, even though we have to give this guy the benefit of the doubt, I personally did not believe him when he said that he did not speak Spanish. What I believe, is that many people of the so-called minorities group become gravely infected with faithless self-denial when emerged in a white society. Their assumed PDMS entraps them under the spell of white supremacy. Therefore, they themselves begin to see different images in the mirror. As far as they are concerned, they have assumed a new identity.

At this particular point, black American people have to stop focusing on the ramifications of slavery as the reason for their current state of affairs. The Jews were enslaved too, but their descendants are not walking around as if still in shackles. Yes, the freed Jewish slaves were allowed to carry their belongings with them; but do not think that the grass is always greener on the other side. Besides, it is not for us to argue with the Father regarding his will. Parents usually say that they love all their children the same. However, the children sometimes become jealous of one another when the parents give them different gifts—each child thinking that the other's gift is better. We have to find remedies for the unhealed wounds.

The symptoms of PDMS among black Americans are obvious to some people of other racial groups. However, they are not quite sure of the causes of these symptoms that have manifested themselves as self-hatred and disunity. Case in point: An Indian associate of mine once asked me why is it that black people in America harbor such dislike for one another; and why they seem to have no regard for the social and economic plight of their people. He said that Indian people have their problems, but at least they have an unspoken unity. He said that they normally have relatively good fellowship and prefer their own kind. That is a statement just about every American can agree with. Indian people believe in working with other Indian people with the hope that their people will eventually own everything. Quite the contrary seems true for the black community. Black people in America will slave themselves away for everyone else, without ever thinking of working together to establish a community that is conducive to the natural progression of all black people. Black American people seem to be more concerned with being accepted by white people—whether that means living in predominantly white neighborhoods, or personal approval—than they are about esteeming their own race.

Black people in America like to brag about living in white neighborhoods, instead of working together to make white, the neighborhoods in which they live—figuratively speaking. Black people in America have a natural tendency to venerate white people, while simultaneously display various levels of disrespect for their fellow black people. Black people will work diligently to build the "white man's" castle—even without a contract; but most will frown at the thought of doing a small favor for one of their own—there is no natural camaraderie.

Black people in America need to avoid becoming too narcissistic and too materialistic; and should try not to focus only on personal achievement and on what they can "get." Rather black people should be focusing more on what they can "give" for the development of a nation of successful people. Each person's agenda should include particular elements for the cumulative growth of black people as a whole. There must be a vision of oneness among American black people.

During the civil rights movements of yesteryear, it seems as if black people were more conscious of their welfare. They might have been more cohesive because of the intense need to triumph over the existing overt racism that was about to destroy our nation. Nowadays, we have what appears to be a phlegmatic movement. We seem to forget the past and we do not show much regard for the future. We have become complacent creatures caught in a clandestine web of covert racism. This clandestine web is spun by the same spider that devoured our people before us. Now, in our equanimity, we have given up the struggle against tyranny. Apparently we believe that we have reached the summit of our existence in America. Therefore, instead of working to fulfill the "dream" of our fore-parents in its entirety, we seem to have a predilection for swimming in uncertainty.

It is easy to believe that black people in America have among themselves, more wealth than the mind can conceive. Yet, as a people, it is perceived that most of us need public assistance to survive. The intolerance for black people that exist in America, does not permit the onlookers to see the great many black people at the top of the social ladder. However, they never fail to see those who cannot even reach the bottom rung. Worst of all, black people themselves sometimes exhibit more intolerance for one another than do Americans of other races.

Yes, there are many wealthy and powerful black people in America; but we as a people cannot judge our success based on the relatively wealthy minority. We have to focus on building a nation of successful people. We even have to try to reach the untouchables of America—those clustered in the inner cities that society has overlooked. We have to try to do whatever we can to *shine them up* so that they can reflect the sun and be recognized. We have to focus on planting seeds of prosperity for future generations. We have to start thinking of becoming great employers instead of becoming great employees. This is of utmost importance—to create a tolerant environment for present and future generations. Black people have been living in these United States for too long to be still living in this continuous state of rejection and maladjustment. Only by conscious decision and concerted effort can we rise above the mockery that we now experience.

As a people we cannot afford to become languid in our journey to attain true liberty. Worse! We cannot afford to become complacent thinking that we have already attained true liberty, just because a few have made it to shore. As a fortune cookie read, "Liberty will not descend upon a people; a people must raise themselves to liberty." White people are not the parents of black people, and it is not their responsibility to make sure that black people receive whatever they need to survive or to have a better life. Black people have to take the responsibility of providing for their own, just like everyone else. Jewish people in America take care of their own affairs; Indian people "look out" for other Indian people. Well, black people need to do likewise, instead of whimpering and pointing fingers and judging the "white man." It is better to turn the focus inward.

Once black people rise above the delusional states of powerlessness and hopelessness, and start to integrate and distribute their natural potentials in American society, then they will procure the desired respect. These natural potentials will develop into natural fruits of success beyond belief. True respect cannot be bought with money; but it can be earned by diligent service that effects necessary change for a better life for all God's creatures.

Black people in America have to wake up and take a walk through the sunlit garden where prosperity resides. In this garden one can experience the fresh air of hope that will displace all fears. In fact, black people need to spend some time together in this garden of hope, and try to develop intimate relationships with one another—that is, we have to learn about ourselves because we know not who we are as a people. We have to wake up from our sour sleep of despair, disunity and subserviency. We have to make an effort to make it on time to the boardroom of reasoning. We have many topics to discuss, and many questions that are "looking" for answers.

It is no secret that black people in America are the least respected of all peoples. Even black people themselves do not generally respect their fellow black people—at least not as much as they respect people of other races. What kind of respect are we talking about? We are talking about just common everyday human decency—the manner in which we treat one another. For example, it is quite obvious to any well-adjusted individual that in many cases, a black person in customer service—a cashier at a supermarket say—normally treats white customers with far more respect than she does black customers. She will smile and greet the white customer favorably; but when the black customer appears in front of her, she holds her head down—no greeting, and no smile. She normally tells the white customer to have a nice day, but not to the black customer. This behavior is prevalent across America, and not just in supermarkets, but in all aspects of customer service. Of course, not all black cashers display this kind of behavior, but it is a large number that do. From a general observation; white cashers tend to be more courteous to all customers. They are more apt to treat black customers equally—depending on the state and the location, however. Could PDMS have developed into a genetic condition that affects a large number of black people?

Black people must realize that exhibiting or showing blatant and unsolicited disrespect for their own kind does nothing but manifest a profound lack of self-respect. This lack of self-respect does nothing but perpetuate the already existing state of inferiority complex that many black people suffer. This lack of self-respect is evident in the inner cities where corner store venders (most of whom are immigrants from poverty-stricken regions of the world) treat their customers, who are usually black, as if they are lower than the dust. What is even worse is that the customers never complain. They accept their bad treatment and move on. They accept treatment from these vendors that they probably would not accept form white vendors anywhere in America. One has to admit nonetheless, that many of these customers display such insane behaviors that the vendors cannot help but treat them according to the character they display. The ultimate manifestation of lack of self-respect is how many black people interact with one another. There is no natural tendency to earn the approbation of one another. Instead, we interact with much distrust and scrutiny. We are just as afraid of ourselves as white people claim to be afraid of us—even though we are afraid to admit it.

Black people have to come to an understanding that they do not have to despise their particular current positions in life, no matter how lowly. Instead one needs to know that one's disposition to ennoble one's position with dignity, integrity, and brotherhood, while maintaining a vision of growth, will bring about a sort of unshakable joy that one can never imagine. Black people will then be capable of walking with the confidence that will help to displace hopelessness.

Before we can attack and eradicate racism, we must first identify its roots. From where did racism originate, and what is the reason for its origination? My theory is that there are two types of racism; (1) active and (2) reactive racism. Active racism is defined as malevolent acts against one who is considered inferior, by another who considers himself the superior. Reactive racism is defined as retaliatory ill will by the afflicted toward the initiator. Active racism is unequivocally far worse than reactive racism because it can give birth to all sorts of insidious afflictions, and is itself responsible for the flare-up of reactive racism.

There is racism everywhere in the world where there is one alleged superior race mingled with other races that are considered subordinates. Even among the so-called subordinates, there is also racism or prejudice of the highest degree. PDMS may play a role in the racism among the people in the alleged subordinate classes because of their constant struggle to win the attention of the people in the alleged superior class.

Within the United States, the focus of racism and racial issues tends to be on white and black peoples. Furthermore, black people have traditionally been the number one recipients of abject racism. Of course, the kind of racism that black people have continually experienced can probably be attributed mostly to the slave-slave master relationship. The relationship that later transformed into a relationship of former slave and former slave master, that was mentioned above. The belief that the slave master had, in that he is the superior being in the relationship, has transcended many generations to today's generation. Therefore, white Americans in today's society generally believe that they are actually superior to black people and perhaps to people of other races. Even if the act of slavery is disregarded—considering that not all black people in today's America are actually descendants of slaves—white people would probably still have the superior mentality due to association.

The burden of this superior mentality that white people carry with them every day, and of which is manifested as racism by those who are psychology and spiritually ill, is actually a condition of the heart. According to the Holy Scriptures, God created humans in his own image—and that means *all humans* (Genesis 1: 26-27). Red and yellow, black and white—he made them all to his delight. So, for one particular race of people or people of a particular color to say that what God made of his own image was a mistake is ultimate blasphemy. Millions of white people attend church every weekend all across America. They attend church to fellowship with God and also with one another. If these people in their most sincere thoughts, think that God loves them any more than he loves black people, and that they are superior to or "better than" black people—then they should know that God hates a proud heart (Proverbs 21: 4; 6:17). They should also know that if they do not extricate themselves from this heavy burden, then the gates of hell are open wide waiting to receive them.

As mentioned before, racism is a psychological and spiritual illness that originates in the heart of man—at least that is my point of view. It is devised or originated to cause disharmony among human beings, which of course is part of the evil plan. Those who think that they are "better than" other people should know that every organ that can be found in their bodies, can also be found in a dog. The main difference, besides obvious physical differences, between a dog and a human being is the divine connection between God and his prized creation— the human being. There is no such connection with a dog. As Jesus Christ tells us, our ultimate purpose on this earth is to live in fellowship with God and with our fellow humans. He tells us that the way to do so is by loving God with all our being and to love our neighbors as ourselves (Matthew 22:37-39).

The reason for comparison with the dog in the above paragraph is to show that there is no extra-special human in today's world. Unless you have the gift to fly as a bird or to create other humans or anything else as phenomenal as these, then you are just like the rest of us—one imperfect human being who can be molded into perfection only by the sacred hands of the Divine Creator. Everyone, regardless of his or her color or race, wakes up with foul breath in the mornings; he or she will be repugnant to everyone else if he or she does not bathe for a few days. So you can be as pompous as you want, but you are not special. You are only as special as other people make you; which is mostly based on material possession that you will eventually die and leave behind. So, in reality, the material possessions that you claim to be yours are not really yours because you cannot take them with you. In effect, you are just stewards. That is why God wants us to humble ourselves, because all things belong to him.

The word of God also said that you show your love for me (God) by the love that you show for your brother: "If a man says, 'I love God' and hates his brother, he is a liar: for he that loves not his brother whom he can see, how can he love God whom he has not seen?" (1 John 4: 20); "And this commandment we have from him (God), that he who loves God loves his brother also" (1 John 4: 21). Of course "brother" is a generic term that means all humans—both male and female. Therefore, by putting it all together, we can see that if for any reason one should express hatred for another, then one is actually expressing hatred toward God, and in effect hatred for oneself. This would be the case because one would be out of fellowship with whomever one hates, and consequently out of fellowship with God, because God is love (1 John 4: 8)—which ultimately leads to self-destruction and condemnation. If one loves oneself, then one does not commit malevolent acts that lead to self-destruction and condemnation.

Reactive racism is just as bad as active racism—as the Holy Scriptures tell us, not to render evil for evil (1 Thessalonians 5: 15). In effect, if black people professed to be victims of racism but reciprocate with similar malicious devices against white people, then who can point a finger? Racism, whether active or reactive, is a very destructive tool. It was constructed with one purpose in mind: To destroy the elemental structures of American societies, which will culminate in the total destruction of the compound unit of America; which of course, will propagate to the rest of the world. America must be the exemplary element of justice of the world. The poem on the following page is dedicated to everyone to everywhere.

Love Thy Neighbor

Sometimes we become so insatiable
That even to ourselves we're unbearable
We wear our clothing of disdain
Which for others can be such a pain
We erect our walls of supremacy
To exclude all inadequacy
We surround ourselves with the best
No need to worry about the rest
We look to the skies with pleasure
While here on earth, we've missed our treasure
We're all guilty of a crime called hate
When one another we try to exterminate
Hate, the termites of our hearts
If not eradicated
We'll forever be segregated
Segregation some may say
Is what we need, come what may
But in our human imperfection
We shall surely see complete destruction
Because it's not in our weakness that we lose
But in our attitude, one toward another that we chose
Many are rich and many are poor
But justice for all we can't ignore
This beautiful world that we're living in
Let's try to make it pleasing
Whether you're black or whether you're white
Let's take the time to do what's right.

Palomino

In order for black people in America to realize true liberty, we have to recondition our minds. We have to dispel from our minds all hatred and bigotry. We have to form new ways of thinking. Black people in America have to first reconcile themselves to one another; and then reconcile any outstanding debt with white Americans. This is not time for supercilious dispositions. Therefore, black and white Americans have to accept the fact that both belong here, and that neither is going anywhere. Just like on the piano, black and white Americans play good tune together. Black and white people can be like complementary pairs.

In a rather atypical way, there are many black Americans who adore and care for their white compatriots. They work together, they go to church together, and they laugh together. By the same token, there are many white Americans who care for and adore their black compatriots the same. Unfortunately, among the great majority there still exists antagonism and intolerance. There stands a wall of supremacy and there lies a precipice of despair that is causing disharmony between the two. How good it would be if we could tear down the wall of supremacy and use its remnants to build up the precipice of despair to form level ground—everyone would have more room to play.

Based on questions that I have asked some white Americans, the problems that they generally have with black people in America are usually based more on physical appearance and social status than on actual color of skin. That is why Americans of Indian descent, even when they are very black, are still more accepted by the general population of white people. As far as physical appearance is concerned, white Americans claim that black people are ugly and have *Brillo Pad* hair. They generally dislike the facial features and the type or quality of hair that black people in America have. As far as social status is concerned, white Americans generally think that most black people are ghetto-like, poor, loud, and have bad odors.

Black people who do not enter much into the world of white America will never know how white people perceive them. All they will probably hear is that white people are racist. For many black people, the first time that they will actually learn what white people really think of them is when they take a freshman sociology class in college. A black person can actually learn to hate himself by the end of the sociology class. That is where he will learn all of the black stereotypes, all of which are extremely negative and downright derogatory; and of course not at all true. I personally believe that, that particular section of freshman sociology should not be taught in colleges where black students are paying their tuition to receive an education. That particular information serves no advantageous purpose whatsoever. Its sole purpose is to propagate hatred and bigotry and infect black students with inferiority complexes.

As far as being loud is concerned, Americans are usually relatively louder than Europeans or most other nationalities. Regardless of race, Americans are generally loud, with both white and black Americans generally being the loudest. One can usually identify Americans in foreign countries because they tend to talk louder than everybody else. So it is unfair to say that black Americans are loud.

Any unwashed person will carry an unpleasant odor, whether he is black or white. If we are comparing black Americans who are homeless and are sleeping on the streets, with suburban white Americans who are living in luxurious homes, then of course black people will be considered dirty and smelly. So who are we comparing with whom to come to this derogatory and preposterous conclusion?

What appears to be strange is the fact that white Americans claim that they dislike the physical features of black Americans; but these same white Americans do not have a problem with black people when they visit other countries. In fact, in Jamaica it is common to see white female tourists, mostly from America, sporting local black men as if they were their most prized possessions. White American men likewise have married many black women from the Caribbean without any reservations whatsoever. So what is the reason for the drastic change when these white people are home? Black Jamaicans have similar facial features and similar quality of hair to black Americans. So there must be something deeper than just physical attributes. As far as social standing is concerned, black Jamaicans who are targeted by tourists are generally quite poor and uneducated.

Could it be that while in Jamaica, these white people do not have to encounter the mostly covert, yet persistent clash between active and reactive racism that is present in America? In other words, while white Americans are in Jamaica, maybe they feel like they are at a good friend's house where they feel quite comfortable and tension free. However, when they are home in America, perhaps it is like being at a family reunion with family members that they totally dislike but have to put up with. In effect, the relationship between white and black Americans is one of constant tension and discomfort. Both usually pretend to be comfortable with each other, but at the end of the day they enter into separate worlds where they have almost nothing to do with each other.

The same level of comfort that white Americans tend to experience with black people in foreign countries tends to transpire here in America as well, as far as interacting with foreign black people is concerned. White Americans are usually more tolerant with immigrant black Americans; and although it is rather strange, nevertheless, they generally prefer to have relationships with black people who speak with accents. They prefer immigrant black Americans than native black Americans.

A white female from a lower-middle-class neighborhood in Philadelphia mentioned that most of the people she knows, as well as she herself, generally hate black people; and that they usually have more tolerance for black people who speak with accents.

When the reason for the disparity was investigated, some native white Americans said that they do not like native black Americans because they generally subtract from the American society. The general perception that many native white Americans have is that immigrant black Americans are usually more productive to the American society. They believe that most of the black people who come to America, especially from African countries and the Caribbean, tend to be more serious about education and work. It is interesting to know that the responses from different classes of white people were quite different. White Americans that were better off were more tolerant with their black compatriots than lower-class white Americans. Some of them (upper class) said that they did not have a problem in particular with upstanding black Americans.

However, lower-class white Americans expressed a somewhat intense hatred for black Americans. Most of them said that they did not want black people in their neighborhoods. The same white female mentioned above, who lives in a lower-middle-class neighborhood in Philadelphia, told me many things that I was already aware of; but she also told me things that I was not aware of. She told me that the white Americans that she associates with, definitely hate black Americans and that they always talk dirty about black Americans. She told me that most black people might think that white people like them, just because white people talk with and smile with them. She said that white people only put on a façade. She went on to tell me that the people in her circles hate Secretary of State Collin Powell; and she was not joking. She did not say that the people in her circles did not care for Collin Powell—she said that they hate him and that there is no way they would ever accept him as president of the United States. Some white Americans say that their hatred for black people is so intense that they usually switch the television channel whenever a black face appears on the screen.

One needs to understand that many of these white Americans who are carrying this burden of hate are not necessarily people who feel superior—but people who actually feel inferior. So, naturally they would hate Collin Powell because they cannot walk beside him. White Americans in this lower class not only hate black Americans but they also tend to despise their fellow white Americans of the upper class. I once caught a white female classmate of mine crying because a fellow white female classmate (of the upper class) whom she wanted to be friends with would not socialize with her. She later told me that she hated certain white people because they think that they are "better than" her. In general white Americans in the lower class are more likely to display antagonistic social behaviors and intolerance—from my observation—probably because of their own insecurities. Perhaps the reason why white patrol officers often stop black motorists driving expensive cars is in correlation with this same line of reasoning.

In general, black people in America do not harbor any ill will toward white people. It appears as if most of what black people in America are demanding of white people are, equal justice, equal rights and respect; none of which that can be bought with money. Therefore, black American people have to work together to build a nation of prosperous and successful people, not necessarily to gain the "white man's respect" but to germinate a people who love themselves. We have to learn to love ourselves again. If you love yourself—that is—if black people are able to love one another regardless of what white people think or try to propagate, then black people would be able to love white people without hating themselves. The result of this accomplishment would be a nation of black people wielding a tool that embodies confidence and self-respect. Black people could now stop seeing themselves as the ugly duckling and start seeing themselves as the elegant swan.

As a people who love themselves, black American people will develop a sense of brotherhood, encouraging and nurturing camaraderie, culminating in a reduction of hatred, bigotry and violence among themselves. As a people we would be more capable of working with white people without losing our identity and self-respect. As far as the open wounds (mentioned above) are concerned, they can never be healed so long as black people defy the precept of "love thy neighbor as thy self." However, one has to love oneself first before one can truly love one's neighbor. So let us talk about finding the right medicine and favorable conditions to heal the foregoing open wounds.

In the darkness everything is dreadfully alive, but only until you turn on the light. So let us turn on the light in America so everyone can see clearly the things that are lurking in the darkness. Native black and white Americans have tolerated this continuous darkness for too long. Each is having a different perception of the images in the darkness, but either is afraid to turn on the light and reveal the true nature of the images. While some things are probably better left in the dark, it is more likely that the light will reveal images that are not so frightening after all, and dispel all built-up fears.

Many native white Americans claim to be afraid of native black Americans or afraid of black people in America in general. However, there is no evidence that black people have been a threat of any kind to white people. Black people are more of a threat to their own kind, shamefully so, than they are to white people. During riots, for instance, black people normally destroy their own environments. I have not yet seen a case where black people marched into white neighborhoods and destroyed them. However, there is evidence whereby white people have marched into black neighborhoods and destroyed them. So, who should really be afraid of whom? Nonetheless, black people should also acknowledge that although there are many active racists in America, that there are also many white Americans who are sensitive and responsive to the plight of black people. So it is really inappropriate for black people to state that white people are racist. Black people should not refer to racism in general terms, but instead should deal with specific issues and specific people. Furthermore, talking about racism all the time without specific plans to resolve specific issues is a waste of time, and serves only to propagate tension and disunity.

Black American people have to understand that before we can apply medicine to the wounds to aid in the healing process, we must first clean up the wounds. We have to clean around the perimeters, and we may even have to irrigate some of the wounds because of the accumulation of dead tissue due to years of neglect.

The first step in the healing process is for black people to dispel the ideology that the "white man" is the superior being. The "white man" is no longer the slave master and the "black man" is no longer the slave. Also, not because one is enslaved means that one has to be a slave. Therefore, black people must retrieve their innate God-like spirit and stand on the same platform with white people. The "black man" must extricate himself from the concept of inferiority and walk in parity with the "white man." This is the first step in the building of self-confidence and self-respect. Once the "black man" sheds his skin of inferiority complex, he can then learn to love the "white man" without hating himself. He will also be capable of accepting the "white man" for all that he is without rejecting himself and feeling the need to be the "white man." This is by no means an easy task since there are so many victims of PDMS. Therefore, we have to work to eradicate PDMS.

In order to eradicate PDMS, we have to seek after wisdom. True wisdom, of course, comes from God and only few seek it; but folly belongs to man, which he wears as a chain around his neck for many to see and envy and kill for. Therefore, we have to diligently ask our Divine Creator for divine wisdom. With wisdom we will come to the understanding that significant life improvements can be measured not only by financial increase but by intangible gains as well. Jesus Christ never had any wealth, yet we worship him. We listen to his teachings and try to abide by his intangible precepts. One of his percepts clearly states that we should let our treasures be in heaven and not here on earth (Matthew 6: 19-21). Nevertheless, many of us judge our success and happiness on our financial gains, and we exclude those who are financially inadequate. The truth is money can buy you only temporary happiness and some amusement. Happiness itself is a byproduct of your daily activities or external influences. So one moment you could be happy, and another moment you could be sad. Naturally if you win millions of dollars in the lottery you are going to be very happy—but for how long? After a lapse of time and you should find yourself without meaningful relationships with either God or your fellow humans, you will not be so happy.

Joy, unlike happiness, however, is anchored on hope. Hope itself is anchored on love. When we believe that God loves us, we will be able to experience joy no matter what our circumstances are. Even when we are sad we can experience joy. This same hope that we have in God can be extended to our fellow humans. When we love one another regardless of our positions in life, then we are able to have hope in one another. Our love should not be restricted to race or color; for if we are wise we must learn to love the diversity of colors around us in which we will find much delight.

Ultimately, in order to eradicate PDMS, black people in America have to start seeing themselves with different eyes and definitely start listening to the voice of the Divine Master and not the voice of the former slave master. The Divine Master said that he created us in his image and that he loves us no matter what our positions in life. With hope in the Divine Creator, we do not have to fear what lies before us. Daniel did not fear the lions when he was thrown into the lions' den because he had hope in the Divine Creator. So there should be no need for black people in America to be infected with inferiority complexes. That in itself is an act of irreverence to God.

The second step in the healing process is for black people to accept the past as a platform to display the courage and strength that black people possess. As a people we have triumphed over the grave and we have passed through the darkness and we are now in the light. Now that we are in the light we are capable of loving those who were once our executioners. It is our duty and our delight to be able to express this kind of love. Hatred and guilt are two kinds of diseases that deteriorate the mind and with time destroy the soul. So we should not allow ourselves to lose twice. We might have lost our freedom in the past, but we should not permit the chance to lose our souls in the present or in the future.

Now that the environmental conditions are more favorable, we can apply the medicine to the wounds. We can start by focusing on prosperity in numbers. We have to build a nation of confident and successful people in large numbers. We have to focus on becoming employers who will create tolerant environments for our people. That means we have to start to instill in the minds of our young the value of college education, and the value of becoming highly skilled professionals in all academic and vocational fields. Black people in America must realize that people of other races are not smarter than they are, and that the only way that these feats can be accomplished is by commitment and hard work with tangible goals in mind. The only way one can become an excellent student in mathematics is by practice;

the same way one would practice for soccer or basketball. That means one would have to do hundreds of problems in mathematics. As my high school mathematics teacher used to tell us, "Whenever you take an examination, you should never see a strange problem." From what I have observed, almost all black people in America think that Asian people or white people are smarter than they are. Black people in America should not forget which voice to listen to.

The only reason why black people in general believe that Asian people especially are smarter than they are is due to indoctrination. That is what they were told, so they believe it. Therefore, because they believe this lie, they feel inferior whenever they are in the company of these people, and tend to give them more respect than they give to their own people. This lack of self-respect causes one to develop low self-esteem resulting in inferiority complex and ultimately in unproductiveness. The truth is, proficiency comes through practice. Therefore, if Asian students do well in school, it is because they practice diligently. Likewise, if black students want to do well in school they also need to practice diligently. Some of the smartest college students that I have met are diligent black students.

Black people in America have to come to an understanding that the problems we have, as a people, are not due to a lack of money. Besides, money alone cannot solve the problems that we have. In fact, without the wisdom required to deal with the current problems, too much money may just exacerbate them. We have to focus first on the intangible gains which will serve as the impetus to attain the tangible gains. We have to focus on healing the wounds by applying the precepts that we have been discussing. After the wounds are healed, we will no longer have any distractions due to pain or sorrow. We will then be capable of participating in all events without fear of being hurt; because we will now be sound in mind, in body, and in spirit. Each person will then be proud to stand on his or her own platform and deliver to the world with confidence, his or her contribution. We must remember to give our gratitude to our Divine Creator for granting us the fortitude to triumph over the grave.

Conclusion

There are some Americans who prefer to identify themselves as African-Americans. As we have addressed certain questions before, let us bring them to the forefront once again. We asked the questions: Is African-American a race? Is African-American a nationality? Is African-American a culture? Is African-American an ethnic group? We admitted that African-American cannot be a race because all black people are not identified by that term. Furthermore, we have agreed that in order to be of the same race we have to have the same racial name or identification because one's race is invariable. Thus, we have concluded that African-American is not a race.

I am quite sure that we can all agree that there is no country on this planet by the name of African-America—at least not this country. Therefore, African-American cannot be a legitimate nationality because one would have to be from or be a citizen of a country by the name of African-America. Besides, since everybody from the same country is technically of the same nationality, and since all Americans cannot categorically be referred to as African-Americans, this further proves that African-American is an illegitimate term. So, no American should be identified as an African-American. Just the sound of the term is painful to the ear because of its alien association.

As far as culture is concerned, African-American cannot be a culture because of the vast cultural diversity among the American black population. Deciding exactly who belongs to African-American culture would be a daunting task, and would prove to be unreasonably idealistic. Incidentally, because of the myriad of cultures that constitute the American black population, such as those incorporating the different cultures from the different countries in Africa; and those from the different regions in the Caribbean; and those from the native cultures of America, etc., a dogmatic African-American umbrella proves inappropriate. Unequivocally, individual cultures want to be, and are expressed, which contest any blanket African-American culture.

There are countless ethnic groups in the American society; and just as with culture that we just talked about, African-American cannot be used as a blanket ethnic group to satisfy all the different ethnic groups of the black population. An ethnic black Dominican and an ethnic black Jamaican are very different; as are an ethnic native black American and an ethnic black Cuban, for instance. Therefore, to classify all black people in America as ethnically African-American is highly inappropriate. In these comparisons, we use the term native black Americans to refer especially to Americans of non-immigrant ancestry because they are indeed native to America. However, it should also include all born Americans.

The people that Americans are now referring to as Native Americans, I prefer to refer to as Original American Natives, just to avoid any further confusion. These distinctions seem to be conceivably less ambiguous and less confusing than the current ones being used. Everyone born in America is a Native American as far as I am concerned. If you were born and raised in a particular country, then you must obviously be a native of that country. A naturalized citizen is a Naturalized American—not a Native American.

One must admit that in America, when it comes to the elucidation of racial, cultural, ethnic or any other of the dividing factors, most people are confused. It seems almost taboo to deal with these subjects. These differences among human beings are really more emphasized here in America than they are in most other countries; and appear to be more complicated to deal with. One thing that should be really clear is that an American should never have a need to say "I'm an African-American," or even "I'm a black American." All that an American should have a need to say is "I'm American." You do not have to label yourself. Everyone can see who you are. Think of how ridiculous it would sound for President Bush to say "I'm a white American," or "I'm a European-American." First of all, everyone can see that he is a so-called white man, and second of all, it would sound really stupid. Notice that he does not refer to himself as a European-American.

In other countries nobody uses an identity prefix. In Jamaica for instance, a black man is a Jamaican; and a white man is a Jamaican; just as well as an Asian man is a Jamaican. All the different races and cultural groups share the common culture and the common language; while some of course espouse their traditional cultures without hindrance. A typical example is the Chinese who celebrate their "Chinese New Year," which is different from the January one New Year celebrated by other Jamaicans. No one usually says (while in Jamaica) I am a black Jamaican or I am a Chinese Jamaican. They are quite sure of who they are, and whatever their race, that is obvious to everyone else. Someone may say "that Chinese guy" or "that white guy" but not usually "that Chinese-Jamaican guy." "That Chinese Jamaican guy" would be more appropriate if the guy were in another country, and especially if identified by someone who is not Jamaican. If there is ever a need for a specific identity, one simply says, "a white guy," or "a Chinese guy," or "a black guy," but people do not normally say "a European-Jamaican," or "an African-Jamaican" or any other absurd combining form.

The real issue here is that American black people need to extricate themselves from all the labeling tools and accept their legacy. American black people are legitimate Americans. As legitimate Americans there should be no need for any American to be referred to as an "X- or Y- or Z-American." The continued use of a particular label such as the one we are currently addressing (African-American), can probably result in confusion, isolation, disparagement, reduction in power and perpetuation of the enmity between American black and white compatriots, and probably among other Americans as well. Therefore, it should be discontinued.

The slave master infected the slaves by virtue of his preferential treatment of some slaves, with a condition called the Puppy Dog Mentality Syndrome or PDMS. This condition kept the slaves divided then and apparently still has an alarming effect today on a large percentage of black people in America and the world. PDMS is still a serious divisive tool today among black people. The so-called "white man" does not have to do much of anything anymore to inflict PDMS, because black people seem to be incurably affected.

The slave and slave master relationship evolved into a relation of former slave and former slave master, by virtue of the Emancipation proclamation. The intolerance of the former slave master for the former slave resulted in active racism which has continued to the present-day generation and is responsible for the birth of reactive racism. However, black people in America have to learn to listen to the voice of the Divine Creator so that they can learn to love themselves again which will make them capable of loving their white compatriots. Once black people are able to love white people without hating themselves, then and only then can they experience true liberty. This is a liberty that white people have long experienced. There are many white people who love black people and many more who have sacrificed their lives for the betterment of black people. There is much evidence to prove that. One does not have to dig deep in history either, because even in the recent civil rights movements, there were white people who were actively involved. Yet, these white people did not hate themselves just because they loved black people.

However, in America and elsewhere in the world, there are far too many black people who suffer from PDMS and who are seemingly incapable of extricating themselves from the inflexibility of loving white people without hating themselves. Many of them are far gone. They are no longer enslaved but they have remained slaves. Therefore, for black people to experience true liberty is a daunting task, but not an impossible one to accomplish if black people will tune their ears to the voice of the Divine Creator who said that he made us in His image.

If black people and white people can come to the realization that they are complementary pairs that add up to one, then much of the hatred and antagonisms will precipitate to nothingness. That is, Black + White = One. Both are needed for the experiment to work, and one is not more important than the other. So, let us live to appreciate each other, black and white together.

Printed in the United States
59415LVS00005B/640-690